BULL'S-EYE!

THE SMART BOWHUNTER'S HANDBOOK

Sage Advice on :

CROSSBOWS
COMPOUND BOWS
BROADHEADS
TARGETS
CLOTHING & GEAR

BONUS FEATURE
BOWFISHING ON A BUDGET

BOB BANFELDER

Broadwater Books
Riverhead, New York

Copyright © 2018 by Robert Banfelder

All Rights Reserved

No part of this publication may be reproduced, distributed, or transmitted in any form or by any means, or stored in a database or retrieval system, without prior permission of the publisher.

Address all inquiries to:
Broadwater Books
141 Riverside Drive
Riverhead, N.Y. 11901-2451

www.robertbanfelder.com

ISBN: 978-1-7326025-0-2

Printed in the United States of America
10 9 8 7 6 5 4 3 2 1

For Donna

Books by Robert Banfelder

Fiction:

The Richard Geist Three Book Series (Trilogy)

Dicky, Richard, and I. A story of madness in the making. A curious mix of a mother's care and cruelty concerning her young son, Dicky Geist, and the precocious boy's metamorphosis into that of a multiple murderer.

The Signing. An account of a clandestine murderous cult monikered the Inner Circle of Friends, led by Richard Geist. Geist and cult members are hellbent on creating chaos and bringing about the eventual collapse of our government.

The Triumvirate. A tale of Neo-Nazism. Three most powerful men covertly control governments around the globe. Fifty-year-old secrets begin to surface referencing Hitler's progeny, the Manhattan Project, and Nazi gold in this mystery within a mystery. It is the genesis of the Fourth Reich.

The Justin Barnes Four-Book Series (Tetralogy)

The Author. A prolific serial killer is the author and architect of a covert operation whose job it is to place government operatives within the ranks of worldwide extremist groups. Justin Barnes, a street savvy Afro-American maverick, searches unrelentingly for the madman who viciously murdered Justin's female cousin.

The Teacher. Justin Barnes, working clandestinely with Suffolk County homicide detectives on Long Island, is assigned to help track down Malcolm Columba's associate, serial killer Professor Clarence Emery. The pair had worked in concert, and Justin is out to stop Emery before he strikes again. A terrifying tale of evil and what it takes to stop it in its tracks.

Knots. Kalvin Matheson, an out-of-work insurance salesman obsessed with immortality and hero worship regarding two notorious serial killers, follows in the footsteps of his two diabolical pals, but with a subtle signature twist, utilizing intricate knots.

The Good Samaritans. In this final four-part series, Justin Barnes, once again, assists Suffolk County homicide detectives as part of a covert operation in tracking down Sep Cramer, a politically well-connected, ruthless serial killer.

****

Trace Evidence. Inspired by the Robert Shulman Serial Killer Trial in Riverhead, N.Y., Robert Banfelder spent every day for 15 months as a spectator to obtain fodder for this novel.

****

Battered. Based on a true story of an abused woman who murdered her husband, Robert Banfelder communicated with abused women, one of whom spent 15 years in prison for her crime.

Nonfiction:

The Fishing Smart <u>Anywhere</u> Handbook for Salt Water & Fresh Water. A concise yet comprehensive angling and on-the-water activities handbook covering spin, bait, fly-fishing, fly tying, clamming, crabbing, kayaking, canoeing, seafood recipes and much more. For novice through experienced anglers. Endorsed by Left Kreh and Angelo Peluso. [black & white photos]

The North American Hunting Smart Handbook: Bonus Feature: Hunting Africa's & Australia's Most Dangerous Game. A concise yet comprehensive small and big game hunting handbook covering guns and bows. Includes upland bird hunting, land management, whitetail tactics and much more. Special bonus feature includes stories of big game hunting in Africa and Australia by seasoned hunters. [color photos]

The Essential Guide to Writing Well and Getting Published: Bonus Feature: Making Decent Money Writing ~ Plus Little-Known Reward-Reaping Benefits. A must-have guide for both novice and veteran writers. This handbook includes tips on how to make money and gain rewards from outdoors writings. Color-coded lessons for easy comprehension.

INTRODUCTION

Who is Bob Banfelder? Bob is an award-winning crime-thriller novelist and outdoors writer as well as a recent recipient of the Lifetime Achievement Award from the publication board of Who's Who in America. He has authored nine works of fiction, two of which were inspired by actual events. Bob has written hundreds of articles for a number of regional and national magazines, covering the main facets of on-the-water-activities: fishing (spin, bait, fly), clamming, crabbing, and boating—including a comprehensive handbook covering these interests. On the hunting forefront, Bob has penned a number of pieces referencing shot-gunning for waterfowl and upland birds; deer hunting whitetails with slug-gun, rifle, muzzleloader, handgun, and compound bow—also including a compendium on these topics. Additionally, he has scribed a succinct yet comprehensive text titled *The Essential Guide to Writing Well and Getting Published*.

Bob has affectionately been monikered the "Jack-of-all-Trades—Master of Fun!" His **KISS** (**K**eep **I**t **S**imple **S**ystem) approach to life, humorously referred to as **K**eep **I**t **S**imple, **S**tupid), is the creed by which he leads a productive existence with his partner, Donna, of forty-six years. On the writing/fishing front, Bob and Donna have been referred to as Long Island's tag-team by Angelo Peluso, noted outdoors columnist, book author, and consummate fly fisherman.

Bob can often be heard saying, "Too many folks love to complicate life. I love to simplify life and offer those folks a moment of peace and joy, which one can readily discover in the great outdoors." That's who Bob Banfelder is.

In this compendium referencing crossbows, compound bows, and bowfishing—along with essential equipment, Bob immediately clears away the cobwebs that might otherwise confuse the beginner. The intermediate or even advanced bowhunter could come away with the finer points when it comes to achieving field-point accuracy when launching both fixed-blade and expandable (mechanical) broadheads via indexing, an often overlooked and debatable subject. Having thoroughly field-tested a dozen popular broadheads and components *simply* designed for unparalleled performance, Bob clearly illustrates and imparts invaluable information.

Bob's credentials are extensive and impressive:

Award-Winning Novelist and Outdoors Writer
Cablevision TV Show Host, *Special Interests with Bob & Donna* [Suffolk and Nassau County, Long Island, New York]
Member: Outdoor Writers Association of America
New York State Outdoor Writer's Association
Long Island Outdoor Communicators Network
Lifetime Achievement Award from Who's Who in America

Complete information is available on Bob's website www.robertbanfelder.com.

AUTHOR'S NOTE

Except for two quality name-brand product models featured in this book, all others are currently available as cited at the time of printing. Manufacturers continuously improve and update their products, resulting in previous models being discontinued For example, Bushnell's quality Legend 1200 ARC laser rangefinder for both gun and bow modes has been replaced with Bushnell's comparable Scout DX 1000 ARC rangefinder. If a model is no longer available, prospective purchasers should research newer models of similar quality under the brand-name(s) discussed herein so as to ensure confidence and consumer satisfaction. The other quality name-brand discontinued item (Plano's soft-sided compound bow case) is covered in the text along with a suggestion on how to obtain one.

CONTENTS

Chapter		Page
I	The Nuts & Bolts of Crossbows	1
II	Crossbow Broadhead/Vane Indexing: The Key to Virtually Achieving Field-Point Accuracy	7
III	Important Information Regarding Crossbows, Broadheads & Arrow Scales	38
IV	Stating A *Case* For Soft & Hard Crossbow & Bolt Cases ~ Expandable (Mechanical) Broadhead Cases	49
V	Stating A *Case* For Hard & Soft Compound Bow & Arrow Cases ~ Accessory Archery Case	57
VI	Targeting Compound & Crossbow Approved Targets ~ Buyer Beware Field Point & Broadhead Targets	62
VII	Selecting Hunting Clothing, Footwear, Bow Accessories For All Seasons	77
VIII	Bowfishing On A Budget: For Beginners & Beyond	89
IX	Bowfishing Reels & Other Essentials	93
X	Rigging An Arrow For Bowfishing ~ 'Switch-Out' Extension-Connections	100
XI	Boats & Beauty Surrounding Bowfishing	107

CHAPTER I

THE NUTS & BOLTS OF CROSSBOWS

Crossbow hunting is becoming increasingly popular as more and more states are permitting and even promoting the sport. In some states (county/zone specific), crossbow hunting may even extend the regular bowhunting season. Of course, there are other good reasons why bowhunters are transitioning from the conventional longbow, recurve, and compound bow to the crossbow. All things being equal, a crossbow's accuracy is, indeed, superior to that of a traditional compound bow. Equipped with a quality scope, a crossbow hunter can confidently harvest game at considerably greater distances than an instinctive archer or one utilizing a compound bow with a peep sight and sighting pin(s).

Another sound reason for transitioning from traditional and/or conventional bows may involve a physically challenging consideration in that it is easier for a person with an impairment to ready a crossbow for firing from the onset than it is to draw back and hold steady a vertically-held bow—especially somewhere between the throes of a trophy lingering before finally presenting itself for a shot. A number of rope- and cranking-type cocking aids make this process possible. Consequently, one can load, aim, comfortably hold, release, and deliver more than sufficient foot-pound force (kinetic energy) with a crossbow. Let's further this last example—leverage being the key.

Placing a foot in the cocking stirrup of a crossbow, one can exert far greater pulling power in cocking and loading the bow via the benefit of arms, legs and back muscles than one could with just the arm-power stroke required in drawing back a vertical bow. A crossbow can easily boast a 170- to 190-pound draw weight whereas a vertical bow might top out at a 70- to 80-pound draw weight. Those differences in draw weight are ostensibly going to give the crossbow hunter a definite advantage. Yes and no. More on that point momentarily. Referencing a vertical bow, when it comes time to shoot, even with 85% let-off and the aid of a release, an archer is not going to be able to draw back and hold indefinitely. However, holding a crossbow like a rifle, especially with a bit of support, whether upon one's knee while sitting positioned in a treestand, lying prone upon the ground, or even standing in an offhand position, a hunter is way ahead of the game (no pun intended). As a result of all these advantages, crossbow hunting is, indeed, becoming increasingly popular.

Bob Banfelder

Clearing Away the Cobwebs of Confusion

This would be a good point to clarify several terms that often lead to misunderstandings among those new to bowhunting, be it with a vertically-held bow (more often referred to the conventional, modern <u>compound bow</u>) or a horizontally-held bow (commonly referred to as a <u>crossbow</u>). As both bows employ a levering system utilizing cables and pulleys [referred to as cams and/or idler wheels] in order to bend the bows' limbs, they are in essence compounds. To further *compound* matters (pun intended), there are what is called in-line Draw-Loc vertically-held compound crossbow configurations on the market. We are going to keep things simple, **KISS** being the creed by which I live: **K**eep **I**t **S**imple **S**ystem, humorously referred to as **K**eep **I**t **S**imple **S**tupid.

The vertically-held compound bow we will be addressing employs a peep sight while the archer uses a mechanical release with which to draw the string and launch an arrow. The horizontally-held crossbow employs a scope, is held like a firearm, and houses a trigger mechanism to release and launch a bolt. Throughout this handbook, I will differentiate between these two bows accordingly.

Next, we should define our terms with regard to broadheads in general. The term 'fixed-blade broadhead' is used today to mean that its blades are fully brandished; that is, openly displayed (exposed), locked solidly in place yet <u>removable</u> and, therefore, generally replaceable. Vintage fixed-blade broadheads are usually referred to as blades that are lastingly locked in place; that is, <u>unmovable</u>. We will be weighing in on current usage and field-testing 2, 3, and 4 fixed-blade style broadheads. Also, we will be field-testing another classification of broadhead referred to as expandable (mechanical) types in which its 2, 3, or 4 blades are more compact, streamlined and partially enclosed within a narrow metal sleeve. These blades open upon impact, flying more like a field-point projectile and, therefore, less subject to the effect of aerodynamics. Achieving field-point accuracy will be the thrust of these initial chapters via field-testing and indexing, which will be explained shortly.

To avoid further confusion, the terms arrow and bolt are sometimes used interchangeably in the industry as they pertain to crossbows. For example, CAMX (a consummate crossbow company) partnered with Black Eagle Arrows and developed the spine matched, indexable CAMX Accuspine arrow, which is actually a bolt designed for the CAMX X330 crossbow. More on those fine bolts and crossbow later. The term bolt, however, does not apply to vertically-held bows (longbow, recurve, compound) and is, therefore, not used interchangeably. Arrows, approximately 30-inches long, are launched via vertically-held bows. Bolts, generally 20-inches in length, are shot with a crossbow. Throughout this handbook, I'll be addressing two types of bows for both target practice and hunting: the vertically-held compound bow and the horizontally-held crossbow. Too, I'll be using the term *arrow* applied to compound bows, and the term *bolt* applied to crossbows—exclusively—except where noted.

Comparisons made between vertical bow and crossbow draw weights are also often misunderstood. My CAMX X330 crossbow with its 165-pound draw weight may ostensibly seem more powerful than my Mathews Z7 Magnum SoloCam vertically-held compound bow with its draw weight of only 50 pounds—when, in fact, they both deliver approximately the same amount of kinetic energy [force upon the target]. Why is that? Without getting too technical, the power stroke referencing my 30-inch arrow is 23 inches; that is, 30 inches minus a brace height [distance between bow string and the deepest part of the bow's grip] of 7 inches = 23 inches. The power stroke referencing my CAMX X330 crossbow is 12.25 inches. Therefore, it requires a more powerful draw weight of 165 pounds in order to load the shorter 20-inch bolt.

Although crossbows have been around since the 6th–5th century B.C., crossbow hunting is a relatively new 21st century endeavor in many parts of this country. Not surprisingly, there is a good deal of confusion when it comes to crossbow selection in general and especially crossbow scopes. One of the first things a prospective buyer should realize is that a crossbow scope can be quite a bit different than one fitted for a rifle, muzzleloader, slug shotgun, or handgun. Why is that? The answer is because *quality* crossbow scopes are specifically designed, calibrated, and may be custom-built for a particular crossbow company. A crossbow scope for target shooting and/or hunting is designed for much closer ranges than firearm scopes. Generally, a crossbow scope's reticles are calibrated in 10-yard increments. For example, 10-, 20-, 30-, 40-, 50-, 60-, and 70-yard distances—not that you *aim* to harvest animals at those greater distances if you're new to the *game*. Until one becomes proficient with a crossbow, by and large, shots are usually limited to 30 or 40 yards—and, as mentioned, with far greater accuracy than a conventional vertical bow and arrow. You wouldn't want to push the envelope by taking an unethical shot and wounding instead of harvesting the animal outright.

Aiming for Accuracy

Crossbow accuracy as it pertains to hunting is comprised of three basic components: crossbow, crossbow scope, and carbon bolts affixed to broadheads. Supreme crossbow accuracy is comprised of a quality crossbow, a caliber crossbow scope, along with spine matched and indexable bolts coupled to broadheads. If there is a superlative to this supreme scenario, it would be the melding of these key components into a calibrated, unified whole. Not every crossbow company can pull off this hat trick. However, CAMX's hunting technology does exactly that.

Let's take a moment and examine the crossbow scope and its relationship to MOA (**M**inute **O**f **A**ngle) accuracy. I'm going to simplify what is often considered a complicated concept, boiling it down to its basics in terms of what you need to know to sight in a crossbow. If you already have a basic understanding of MOA as it pertains to a rifle scope, you may be surprised to learn that it can be quite different when applying the formula to a scope specifically designed for a crossbow. The whole MOA concept is confusing at first blush. I facetiously refer to MOA as the

Mother **O**f **A**ggravation. However, I will briefly examine this concept in its simplest terms. It's really pretty simple when applied to scopes designed for crossbows.

To understand Minute Of Angle, picture a pie, a circle, or better yet, the face of a clock—which, of course, is divided into 60 minutes. As a circle or the face of a clock is comprised of 360 degrees, one Minute Of Angle represents 1/60th of that one degree. This translates into capable <u>firearm</u> accuracy of <u>1 MOA equaling approximately 1 inch at 100 yards</u>. I say *approximately* 1 inch because the actual measurement is 1.047 inches at 100 yards—a far greater distance than what we'll be concerning ourselves. We'll be hunting game with a crossbow, up close and personal, not sniper-shooting considerable distances in Afghanistan or Iraq with a rifle. The MOA formula is a given rule for the intended purposes of firearms, not necessarily scopes for crossbows. A case in point will follow shortly. But first a brief understanding of MOA scopes in general.

Most MOA scopes are generally calibrated in one of three settings: 1 MOA, ½ MOA, or ¼ MOA. The most common is the ¼ MOA scope. Again, keep firmly in mind that crossbow-designed scopes can be quite different from firearm scopes, shooting distances being the distinguishing factor. Yes, a rifle scope may work on a crossbow—but rather inadequately.

Let's assume that a rifle scope is ¼ MOA. Again the rule is 1 MOA equals 1 inch of movement with each click of the turret adjustment knob at 100 yards. Therefore, the crosshairs/dot reticles of a ¼ MOA rifle scope are going to move the point of impact one quarter that distance; that is, ¼ inch per click at 100 yards. As most crossbow scopes are zeroed in for 20 yards, you are five times closer to the target. That would normally equate to turning the turret knob 20 clicks for each inch of movement at that 20-yard distance <u>referencing a rifle scope</u>. However, you will be utilizing a <u>crossbow scope</u>, not a rifle scope. What to do.

The Scoop on Crossbow Scopes

For the purpose of clear, concise explanations and illustrations, I'll be using components found on the CAMX X330 crossbow; my crossbow of choice. For openers, the crossbow's 4x32 ARC (**A**rrow **R**ange **C**ompensation) 330 scope does not follow the rule referencing the 1 MOA formula covered earlier because it is a specifically designed crossbow scope utilizing 1¼-inch MOA turret adjustments for windage and elevation, which equate to ¼ inch point of movement at 20 yards. Therefore, I need only make a 4-click turret adjustment for 1 inch of movement at 20 yards—*not* 20 turret clicks as I would normally need to make for a ¼ MOA rifle scope sighted in at 20 yards. Got it? Good.

CAMX's 4x32 ARC 330 crossbow scope is mounted on a solid one-piece precision machined aluminum Monobloc base foundation, utilizing a 1½-inch eye relief, not the usual 4-inch eye-relief distance found on most rifle scope receivers. All-steel Weaver-style scope rings secure the crossbow scope to the Monobloc for unparalleled accuracy. Too, the Monobloc houses CAMX's ingenious PAR (**P**ivoting

Arrow **R**etention) system. For purpose of demonstration, the crossbow with a loaded bolt held within the retaining clip, pointed in a vertical position, then smacked forcefully on the ground upon the bow's stirrup several times, would not drop the bolt. All this technology translates into flawless accuracy and all-weather functioning.

The wizard behind the curtain is crossbow designer Dave Choma, a man who cuts no corners when it comes to building CAMX crossbows. The company's slogan is "Built Like No Other." As a first impression, one might think that this boast is a bit of hyperbole. Let me assure you that it is not an exaggeration in any way, shape, or form. One has only to view the videos listed on the menu in the upper right-hand corner of their website, www.camxcrossbows.com, to witness that this is the gospel. You won't believe your eyes! Paul Vaicunas, vice president of CAMX Crossbows, et al, clearly explain and demonstrate that this crossbow *is*, indeed, built like no other. For openers, Paul drops then hurls the crossbow across a concrete floor (not the floor of a forest where a mishap might occur) retrieves the bow and shoots a bull's-eye. Paul is one of the best presenters I've seen, leaving no stone unturned in explaining the innovative technology behind this remarkable product.

Turret: Crossbow scope turret indicator

A simple formula for the 1¼ inch (1.25) Minute of Angle (MOA) turret adjustment knobs (not ¼ inch) is 4 – 1 – 20; that is, 4 clicks = 1 inch of movement at

20 yards.

Therefore, if I am shooting 1 inch too high at 20 yards, I simply adjust the elevation knob 4 clicks down.

If I am shooting 2 inches to the right at 20 yards, I simply adjust the windage knob 8 clicks to the left.

If I am shooting ¼ inch to the left at 20 yards, I simply adjust the windage knob 1 click to the right.

If I am shooting ½ inch to the left at 20 yards, I simply adjust the windage knob 2 clicks to the right.

If I am shooting ¼ inch too low at 20 yards, I simply adjust the elevation knob 1 click up.

Once I am sighted in for 20 yards, my crosshairs/dot reticles are calibrated for 10 through 70 yards. Simple enough? You bet.

Note: It is <u>very important that you read</u> *your* <u>owner's manual</u> to know what turret adjustment *you* have relating to elevation and windage.

Let's move on to the next chapter referencing achieving field-point accuracy with a crossbow when employing broadheads and bolts.

CHAPTER II

CROSSBOW BROADHEAD/VANE INDEXING: THE KEY TO ACHIEVING FIELD-POINT ACCURACY

Field-testing & indexing first set of broadheads

Left to right: precision field point ~ Slick Trick fixed 4-blade ~ Rage X expandable 2-blade ~ SpitFire Maxx expandable 3-blade ~ Wac 'Em expandable 3-blade

In a step-by-step field-test, we will be closely examining a dozen popular crossbow broadheads that fall into a fixed-blade category as well as the expandable (mechanical) classification. For the sake of clarity, we'll arrange them into three groups using two crossbow-approved broadhead targets so as not to crowd the target (graphic) of a whitetail deer. Our bull's-eyes will be red half-inch diameter stick-ons; actually, $5/8^{th}$ inch—rounded to ½ inch for the sake of simplicity. Although the kill-zone diameter of whitetail deer is generally considered to be the equivalent of a 9-inch pie plate, I will use ½-inch red stick-on bull's-eyes accompanying Birchwood Casey Shoot·N·C Targets, with which I practice at the rifle range. Even with a crossbow, I demand and command this kind of accuracy.

Bottom left-hand corner: Birchwood Casey Shoot·N·C Target ~ red ½-inch stick-on bull's-eyes

All things being equal, expandable (mechanical) broadheads fly truer than fixed-blade broadheads. In other words, expandable broadheads fly more like field points, which are, of course, bladeless. Folks who are relatively new to bowhunting—be it with a long bow, recurve, compound, or crossbow—soon realize this fact. The reason is that expandable broadhead blades are retracted to a degree within and along a streamlined projectile (ferrule) and are, therefore, not as subject to the effects of aerodynamics.

If the above is true, and it certainly is, the question arises: Why use fixed-blade broadheads in the first place? The answer is that there are important factors to consider other than spot-on accuracy, which we'll cover shortly. The thrust of this chapter is indexing; that is, properly positioning a broadhead's blades with an arrow's vanes (fletchings) in order to achieve greater accuracy.

The field point and broadheads used in this field-test are 100 grains. The bolt (a.k.a arrow) is a CAMX Accuspine by Black Eagle. Indexing (desired alignment of blades/vanes) is easily achieved with the bolt's components [insert and setscrew] and an Allen hex key. CAMX Accuspine/Black Eagle bolts are fletched two degrees right for ultimate flight performance. All shots are executed outdoors from a precise 20-yard distance under optimum conditions—virtually no wind. The first broadhead we'll field-test is a **Slick Trick fixed 4-blade**, followed by 2- and 3-blade expandable broadheads.

In shooting my CAMX X330 crossbow, practicing with 100-grain field points from distances of 20–30 yards, I'm spot-on accurate after indexing. If I didn't remove the bolt from the bull's-eye following each shot, I would likely damage the former because the CAMX X330 crossbow is guaranteed to shoot 1-inch groups at 20 yards (or less)—and it does. I'm consistently shooting ½-inch and 1-inch groups at 20 and 30 yards, respectively.

For our field-test, I'll be using The Cube Hybrid by American Whitetail Systems with its optional inner compression foam core cap—specifically designed for broadheads.

The Cube Hybrid with optional inner compression foam core for broadheads

To maintain spot-on accuracy employing field points at 20 yards, the CAMX X330 crossbow, equipped with a 4x32 ARC crossbow scope, is secured upon a rock-solid Bulls Bag X7 shooting rest atop an equally rock-solid table.

Author with CAMX X330 Crossbow equipped with telescopic sight, CAMX Accuspine/Black Eagle Bolt, rock-solid table platform, Bulls Bag X7 shooting rest system—makes for greater accuracy

Before indexing, let's note the results when I initially fired a 4-blade, 100-grain Slick Trick crossbow broadhead aimed at the ½-inch stick-on red bull's-eye placed upon The Cube Hybrid crossbow target. **Shot #1** hit 2-inches low and 1-inch to the right from the center of the bull's-eye. After making a different blade/vane alignment (indexing), **shot #2** dropped an inch. So as not to crowd the image and confuse the issue, I'm then experimenting with other blade/vane adjustments while shooting at another target in order to achieve the best possible performance from the 4-blade broadhead. Keep in mind that we're dealing with four blades and three vanes, using *the* very same bolt after each shot.

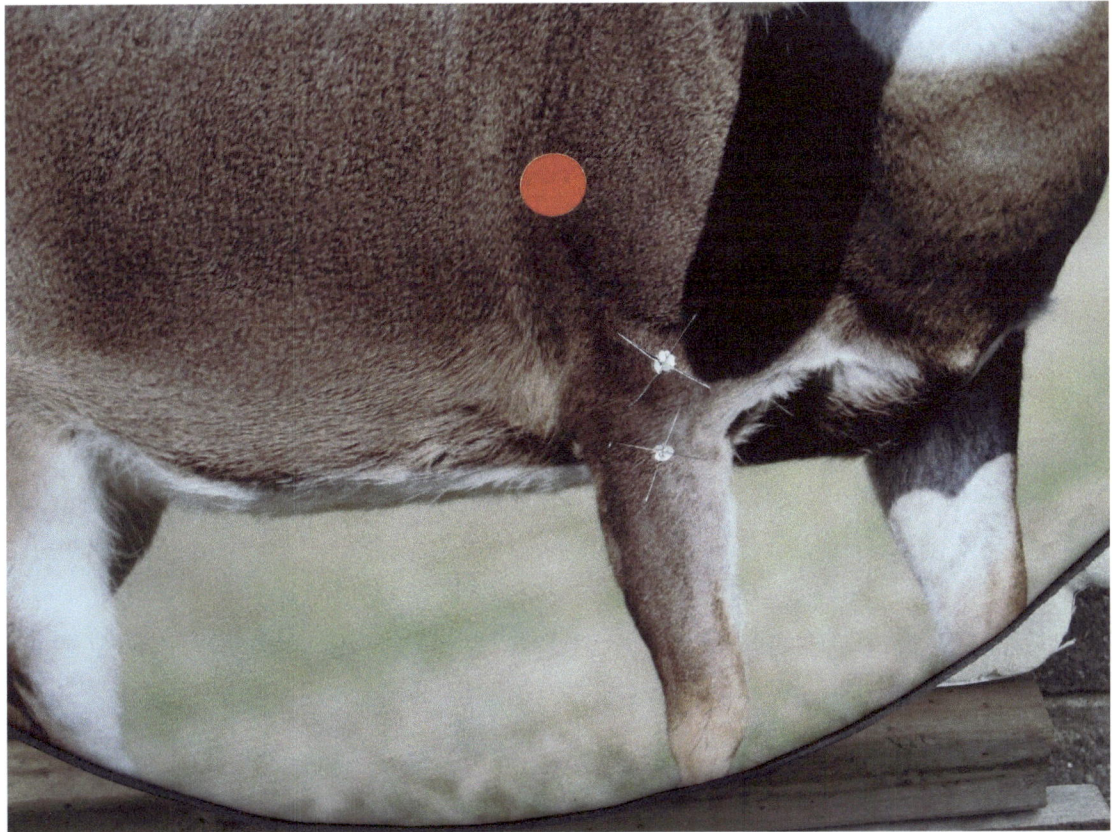

First and second shot launching bolts with a 4-blade Slick Trick crossbow broadhead at ½-inch (red) bull's-eye

    Crossbow, bolts, and Slick Trick broadheads are all part and parcel to the CAMX X330 hunting package. That is why I started with this setup. Let me be perfectly clear at this point. You do not have to shoot a CAMX X330 crossbow to fell deer with pinpoint accuracy. Another quality crossbow will certainly get the job done. However, I strongly suggest launching CAMX Accuspine/Black Eagle bolts with their easily indexable Lock-n-Load inserts for the ultimate in accuracy. Apart from arrows designed by 3Rivers Archery for longbow and recurve bows, as of this writing, I know of no other Lock-n-Load crossbow bolt on the market that has this simple, indexable capability.

    A well-tuned bolt *can* fly with virtual field-point accuracy employing a well-tuned quality crossbow. The bolt's magic rests in its geometry, weight design, and distribution. So then why was my 4-blade Slick Trick broadhead missing the mark (the red bull's-eye), the first shot hitting 2 inches low and 1 inch to the right of the bull's-eye as shown; second shot hitting another inch lower—3 inches away from the bull's-eye? The answer lies in the alignment between the bolt's three vanes and the 4-blade broadhead. The beauty of CAMX's Accuspine/Black Eagle bolts is that they are easily indexable. When the blades of the Slick Trick broadhead and vanes of the bolt were properly aligned—through trial and error at another target so as not to crowd the graphic—the bolt flew closer to the bull's-eye, but still not with the accuracy of a field point.

We'll continue with the 4-blade Slick Trick broadhead coupled to the CAMX Accuspine/Black Eagle bolt. These 20-inch carbon fiber crossbow bolts are spine indexed and matched, meaning the specifications of each bolt are held to exacting tolerances: Diameter (0.344 inch), ID (0.300 inch), Wall (0.022 inch), Shaft Weight (9.1 grains per inch), Straightness (+/- 0.001 inch), Deflection (+/- 0.010 inch), FOC (**F**ront **O**f **C**enter) balance point (17.7%), Total Weight (410 grains including 92 grain Lock-n-Load brass insert plus 100 grain field points or broadheads). Indexing offers the do-it-yourselfer the choice of where to precisely align broadhead blades and vanes. With CAMX Accuspine/Black Eagle bolts, no longer does the archer require the involved procedure of grinding down injection shafts or the archaic process of employing a heat gun and melting glue in order to align blades/vanes. CAMX Accuspine indexable bolts allow for a more uniform flight. There are naysayers out there who debunk this concept. However, in a moment, we will clearly see that tuning broadhead blades to align with a bolt's vanes in a given position is the key to greater accuracy.

One can easily adjust the vanes of CAMX Accuspine/Black Eagle bolts with the blades of a broadhead by either rotating or removing the Lock-n-Load glue-less brass insert from the arrow shaft with a 5/64th-inch Allen hex key. The insert is held fast with a threaded setscrew. Loosen the setscrew to rotate the insert or, better yet, remove the setscrew to facilitate indexing. This way, you are assured that the setscrew will not interfere with the threaded end of the broadhead when reinstalling.

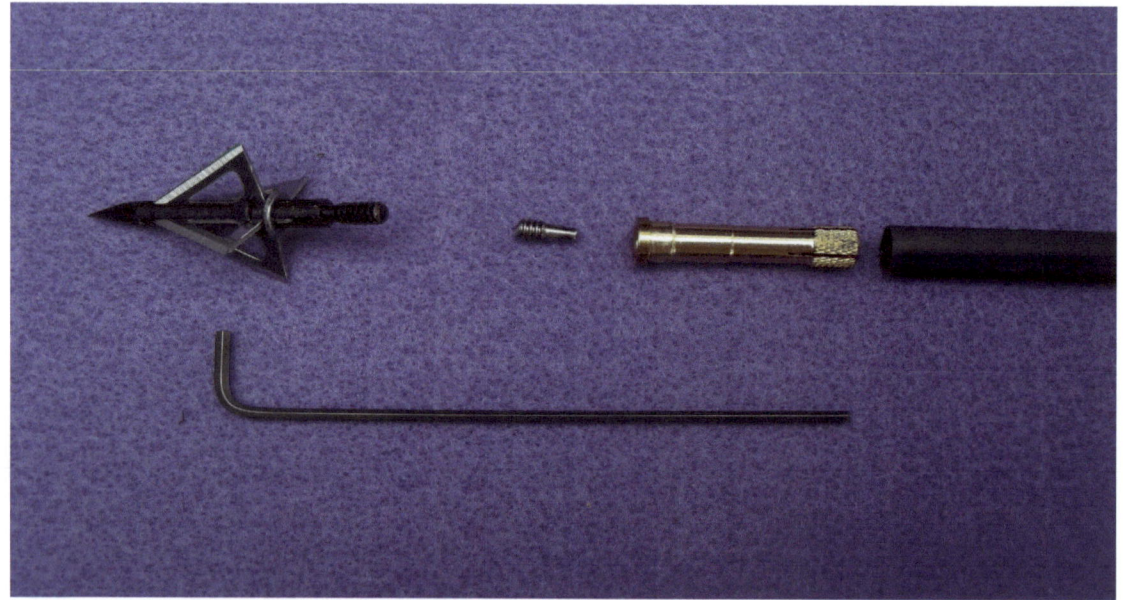

Indexing (tuning) broadhead/bolt made easy: 4-blade broadhead, setscrew, brass insert, bolt shaft, 5/64th- inch Allen hex key

With the setscrew removed, screw the broadhead into the brass insert within the shaft then rotate the broadhead to the desired position. With a fine-point marker, mark the head (tip) of the shaft and the rim of the insert where you want the alignment set. Unscrew the broadhead from the insert, screw in and tighten the setscrew (torque setting of 0.5 foot-pounds) then reinsert and screw in the broadhead. You may note a slight protuberance (bulge/swelling) when you torqued down the setscrew. This is normal, as the setscrew, acting as a collet, expands the rear of the insert to lock in and index the newly aligned position for consummate concentricity. If you need to erase the mark made with the pen to start anew, simply use a small piece of Mr. Clean Magic Eraser.

Indexing broadheads for precise alignment

As there are four blades that form this Slick Trick 100-grain crossbow broadhead, along with three conventional plastic vanes referencing the CAMX Accuspine/Black Eagle bolt, where does one properly align blades and vanes for optimum performance? When I had initially aligned the odd red-colored plastic vane (cock fletch) along the arrow shaft at different points between the **V**, formed by two blades, accuracy suffered as shown by the first and second shots. That is, I was hitting low and to the right of the bull's-eye. However, after I had indexed the cock vane to align precisely with a single blade, performance improved *somewhat*. Elevation went up an inch as you will note in **shot #3**; however, I was now hitting ½ inch further to the right of the first two shots.

After indexing Slick Trick broadhead blade with cock vane. Close, but no cigar.

Making no new adjustment, **shot #4** sent the broadhead into the same hole as the third shot [depicted on the following page], which made clear that the indexed adjustment was consistent and had improved accuracy in terms of elevation. This eliminated any issue of seemingly erratic arrow flight. Again, I experimented with blade/vane alignment at another target so as not to crowd the graphic presented here. The third and fourth shot at the display target was as good as it was going to get with the Slick Trick 4-blade broadhead. Aligning a blade between vanes had resulted in poor performance—the effect of aerodynamics magnified. Precisely aligning a single vane (in this case the cock feather; i.e., vane) with a broadhead blade allowed for greater accuracy, but still not with the precision of a field point. However, that popular fixed 4-blade broadhead hit well within a kill-zone diameter of a pie plate, the red ½-inch bull's-eye serving only as a reference point and not precisely where you would align the crosshairs on the animal for a broadside shot—perhaps a quartering away shot from a treestand.

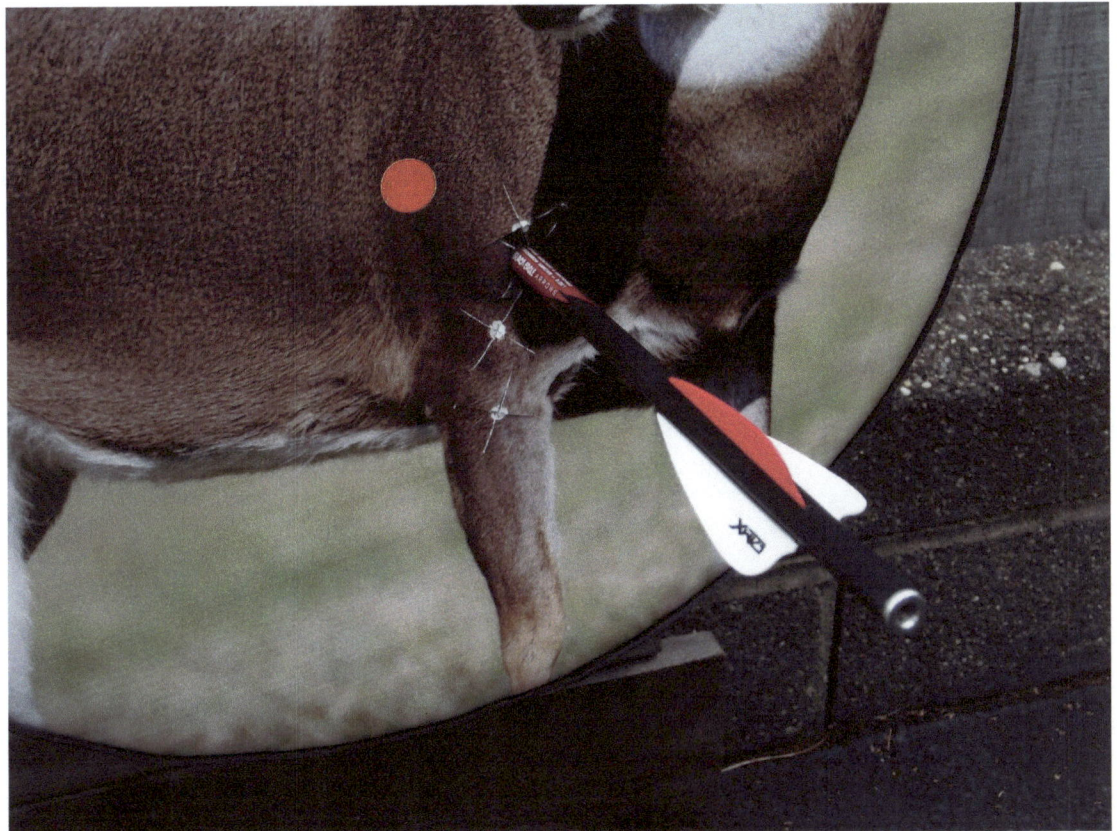

Slick Trick broadhead smacked through the same hole as the third shot

Although you do not normally fire field-tipped bolts into The Cube Hybrid's optional inner compression foam core specifically designed for broadheads—deeper penetration and, therefore, difficult bolt removal being the issue—I wanted to show a clear comparison in that the field-point missile was still hitting with dead-on accuracy. Using the same bolt, I removed the broadhead and screwed in the 100-grain field point. You'll note the result of **shot #5**: Bull's-eye!

Please disregard the next shot shown at the right edge of the dark oblong shadow imprinted on the graphic. A neighbor came by with a half dozen blue-claw crabs and begged to have a shot. How could I refuse?

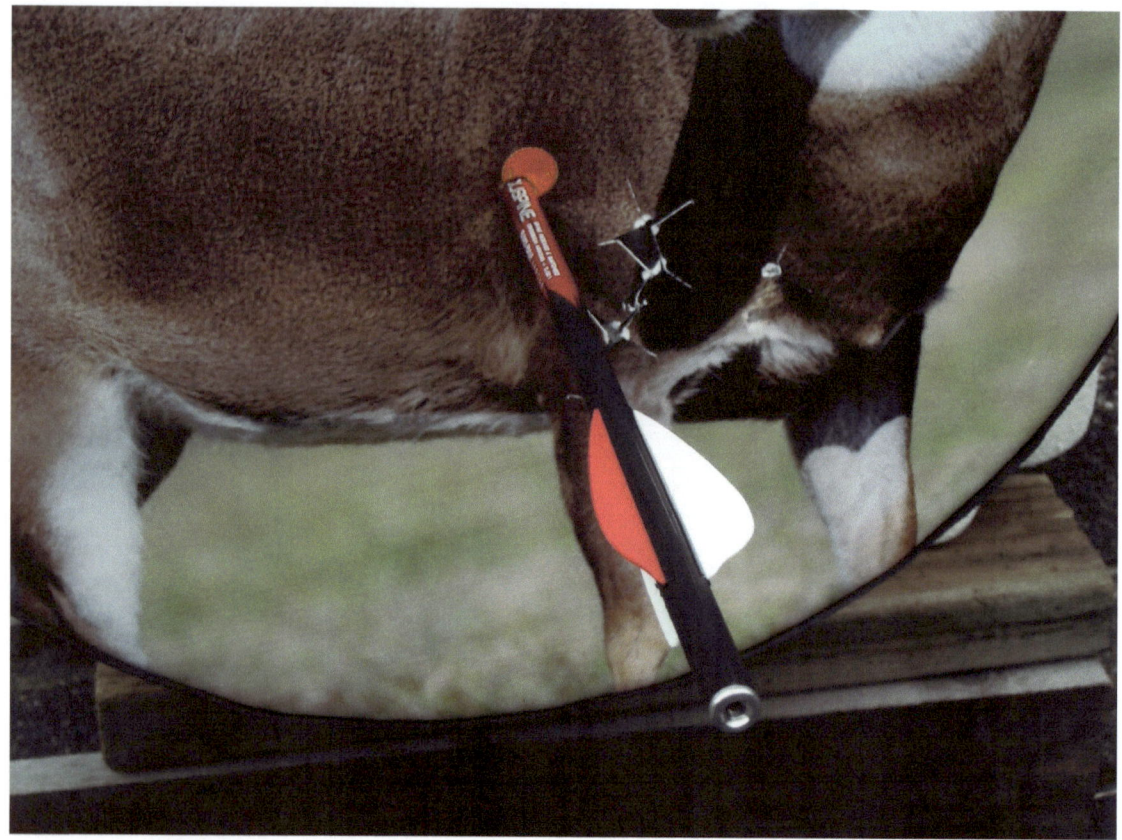

Back to utilizing a 100-grain field point with the same bolt to show a clear comparison. Bull's-eye!

Let's now note how a **Rage X 100-grain 2-blade expandable broadhead** performed as compared to the 4-blade Slick Trick broadhead we've been field-testing up to this point. I've tuned the bolt via broadhead/vane indexing, aligning the cock vane with one of the blades. Note that <u>**shot #6**</u> hit ½-inch directly below the bull's-eye —a far better performance than the Slick Trick 4-blade broadhead.

Rage X Crossbow 2-blade expandable (mechanical) broadhead

Let's move ahead. After properly indexing NAP's (**N**ational **A**rchery **P**roducts) **SpitFire Maxx 100-grain 3-blade expandable crossbow-designated broadhead**, let's see how it fared against the Rage X expandable 2-blade broadhead. Cock vane was again aligned with a single blade. Note that the Spitfire Maxx broadhead struck the top of the bull's-eye in <u>**shot #7**</u>. As both hits are vertically aligned with the bull's-eye, the SpitFire Maxx clearly the winner, which broadhead might you choose? Let's first examine two important factors before deciding: cutting diameter and penetration.

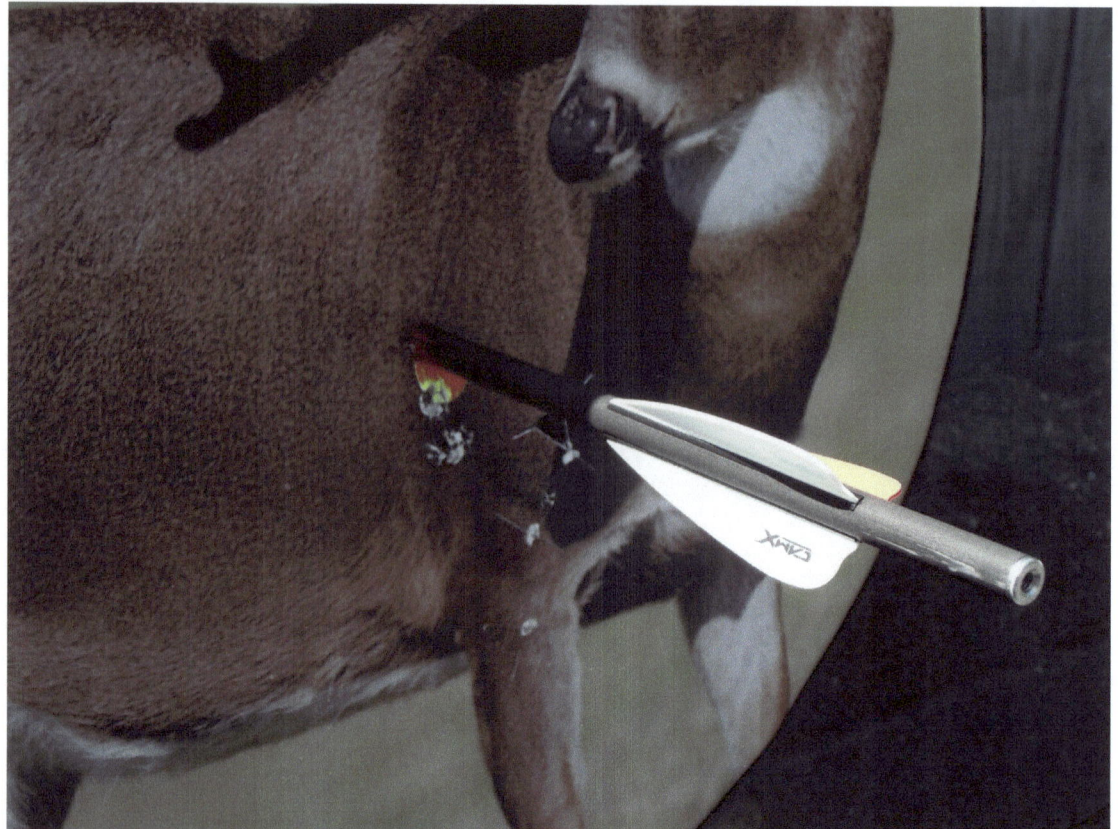

NAP's SpitFire Maxx 3-blade expandable broadhead

Indexing SpitFire Maxx Broadhead

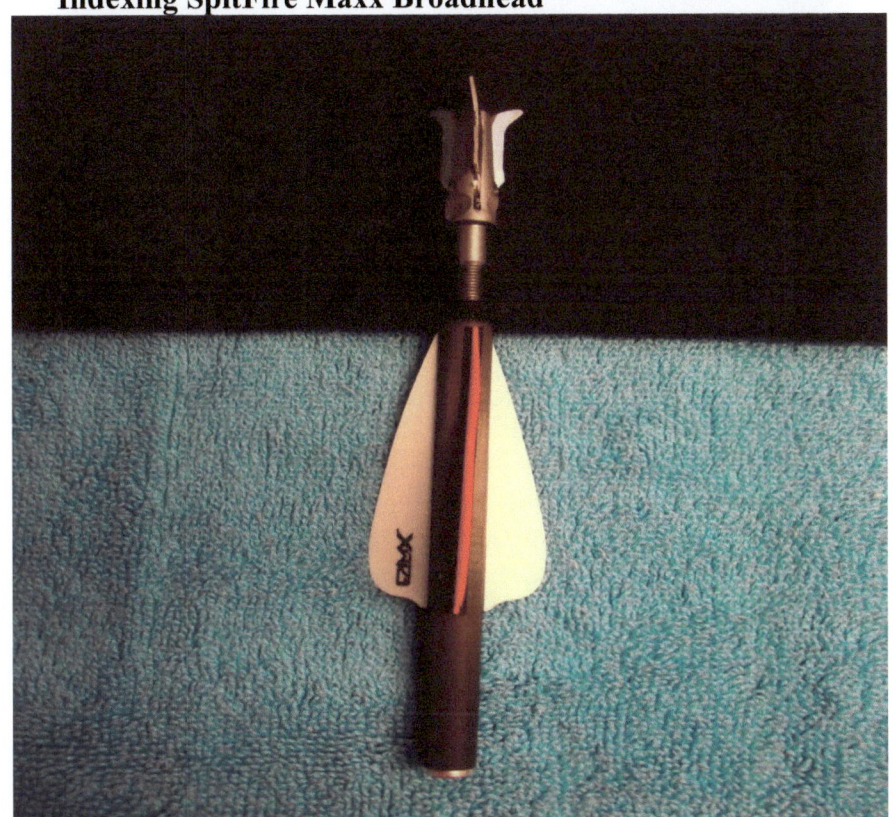

Showing split image referencing proper alignment of the expandable 3-blade SpitFire Maxx crossbow broadhead & CAMX Accuspine/Black Eagle bolt. Cock vane perfectly aligned with a single blade

The cutting diameter of the Rage X 2-blade broadhead is 2 inches, while the cutting diameter of the 3-blade SpitFire Maxx is 1¾ inches, a difference of ¼ inch, but with three cutting edges instead of two. Another consideration is penetration. Broadhead penetration of the Rage X was 10¾ inches; penetration of the SpitFire was 11 inches; again, the difference of ¼ inch. Between these two fine crossbow broadheads, blade thickness, too, is still another consideration. Rage X .035 inch; SpitFire Maxx .030 inch—a difference of .005 inch. Accuracy, number of expandable blades, cutting diameter, penetration, and blade thickness are all elements of consideration and should be weighed carefully. At this juncture, it's pretty much a toss-up between the two expandable (mechanical) broadheads. My point is, just don't make your decision based solely on pinpoint accuracy. Referencing penetration, remember that a crossbow broadhead-approved target is built to stop arrows. In the field, however, for the most part, these bolts are going to pass through the animal save a bone-stopping barrier. A whitetail's rib cage will prove little problem. In the final analysis, a significant blood trail will tell the tale. Both are fine broadheads that will get the job done nicely.

Let's move on to field-testing the fourth and final broadhead in this first group before moving ahead. I indexed the **Wac 'Em 100-grain 3-blade expandable broadhead** by aligning the cock vane to a single blade as I did the others to achieve peak performance. Keep in mind that I had, through trial and error, field-tested and re-field-tested these bolts in various blade/vane alignments on other targets—always with the same results. Performance diminished when I aligned a single blade (simulating the front site of a firearm) precisely between the **V** of the vanes (resembling a rear sight), once again with a single blade just off to either the left or right of center. However, when blade and vane were perfectly aligned, performance improved overall.

Laying the hen vanes (same two-colored vanes) flat upon a table will aid in aligning the cock vane with a blade. You'll note that **shot #8** struck ½-inch from the edge of the bull's-eye. As the Wac 'Em 3-blade expandable broadhead boasts a large 2-inch cutting diameter in addition to a three-pronged leading-edge cutting tip, which is perfectly aligned with its blades, this broadhead is certainly on a par with both the Rage X and the SpitFire Maxx. The Wac 'Em's stainless steel blade thickness is .034 inch.

Wac 'Em 3-blade expandable broadhead hit just to the right of bull's eye

Indexing blades/vanes is your key to approaching and even achieving field-point accuracy. Too, I always opt for a broadhead that is specifically designated for crossbows so as to obtain optimum performance.

Before moving on to field-testing a second set of broadheads, let's take a brief look at a couple of items that will make life easier when shooting into The Cube Hybrid crossbow approved field-point target. An arrow puller such as Red Hot's Lumenok Extinguisher makes removal a bit easier. The target is extremely durable and will survive not hundreds but thousands of shots. The optional inner compression foam core broadhead target should endure hundreds of shots provided that you utilize its entire surface. It's another reason why I strategically place half-inch red bull's-eyes around its face.

Red Hot's Arrow Puller/Lumenok Extinguisher & The Cube Hybrid

Tip: An after-market 4-foot bungee cord laced around and through The Cube Hybrid cover's bungee loops prevents its ends from slipping into the cylinder when inserting the inner compression foam core specifically designed for broadheads. When shooting field points, you'll simply remove the longer bungee cord.

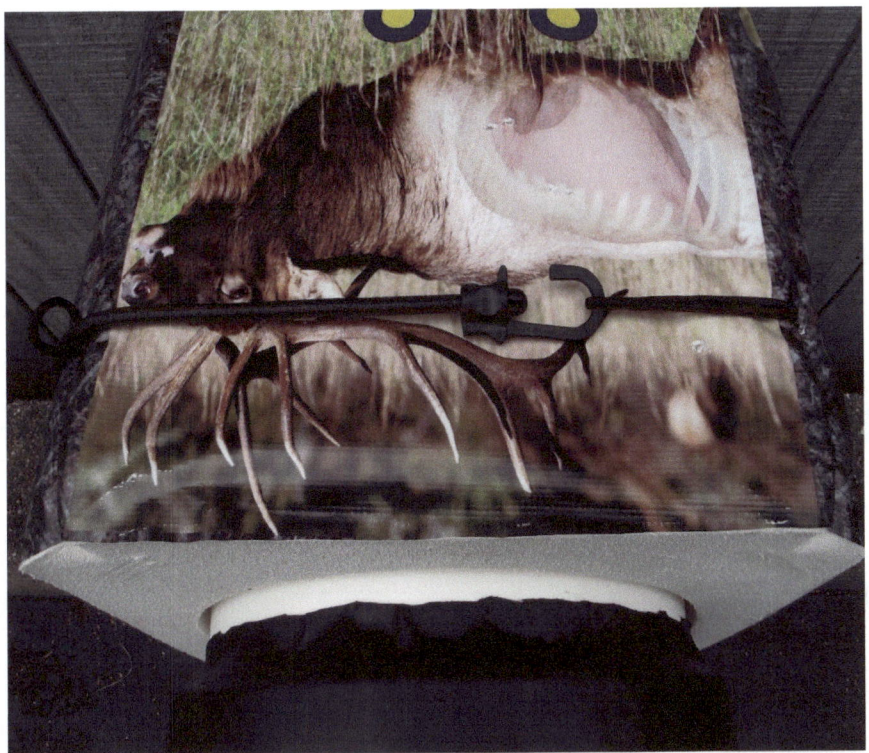

4-foot bungee cord laced around and through the loops of The Cube Hybrid

Field-testing & indexing second set of broadheads

Using the same broadhead target and graphic, but with another ½-inch red stick-on bull's-eye placed to the left of the first so as not to crowd the graphic, let's move on to indexing and field-testing a second group of 3- and 2-blade crossbow broadheads—also from well-known manufacturers. Again, for illustration purposes, the red ½-inch bull's-eye serves only as a reference point and not where you would align the crosshairs of your crossbow scope on the animal for a kill-shot; that is, at its vitals.

Left to right: Wac 'Em fixed 3-blade ~ Muzzy fixed 3-blade ~ Rocky Mountain Warhead X expandable 2-blade

After properly indexing the **Wac 'Em 100-grain fixed 3-blade broadhead** then launching the CAMX Accuspine/Black Eagle bolt, you'll note that <u>**shot #1**</u> hit 1¾-inches to the right of the new red bull's-eye. Not nearly as impressive as the Wac 'Em expandable 3-blade broadhead shot in the first group. Subsequent shots at another target showed the same results. After experimenting via other alignments, the initial indexing of blade/cock vane alignment proved Wac 'Em's fixed 3-blade broadhead as giving its best performance. Again, not so impressive; however, bolt penetration ran 12½ inches deep. Cutting diameter is 1¼-inches; blade thickness .030 inch.

Shot #1: Wac 'Em fixed 3-blade broadhead

Referencing both my Mathews compound bows, arrows, and broadheads, I had been shooting Muzzy broadheads for a good part of my adult life, initially putting them on the back burner because new technology came along years ago, namely expandable (mechanical) styles, promising field-point accuracy. The problem was that like most anything new, issues arose regarding reliability. There were reports of blade deployment failure upon impact. Conversely, there were reports of blades deploying while in flight, a broadhead's plastic band or rubber O-ring that held the blades in place being compromised. As the technology advanced, confidence grew among more and more hunters. Compact, streamlined warheads flew with deadly delivery. Cutting blades grew to unprecedented proportions (e.g., creating gaping 2-inch holes), the negative effects of aerodynamics upon blade surface areas diminishing to a significant degree because blades were now machined to shed weight and virtually housed within the projectile.

But there are those who remained faithful to undeniable fixed-blade dependability, coupled to the kinetic force delivered behind a fully deployed broadhead from the onset. The choice between the two styles (fixed and expandable) is largely based on hunters' experiences afield, relating to his or her successes as well as failures. Those encounters are firmly embedded in one's mind. Both types of broadheads have their place. Shot placement is, of course, what it's all about. Aiming for and delivering *pinpoint* accuracy in lieu of 'close is close enough' target acquisition is a mentality on which you alone should decide. In comparing bone punishing trocar-type tips with leading-edge styles, it is worth pointing out that it would be wise to go with fixed-blade broadheads for large game animals such as elk and moose. Once again, it all goes back to shot placement. Too, I choose to cull smaller deer from the heard for the table and freezer. I already have my trophy buck hanging over the fireplace.

Of course, you could simply practice with your best performing fixed-blade broadhead, making a scope adjustment so as to place every bolt into the bull's-eye. For me, I prefer to practice with field points then select my best performing expandable broadhead for the hunt that truly shoots like a field point. No need to adjust and readjust my scope between practicing with field points then broadheads. I can practice for hours, enjoying easy bolt removal via field points, whereas, truthfully speaking, bolt/arrow removal employing broadheads—even with quality dedicated broadhead targets—can soon take its toll on body and blades.

Either style of broadhead will do its job when hitting an animal's vitals; that is, the thorax cavity comprising lungs, heart, and liver. If you hit a shoulder blade (scapula), you might wish you had launched a solid fixed-blade type broadhead, preferably with a trocar tip. But for more uniformity in flight, especially on smaller size game animals like whitetails, the expandable (mechanical) broadheads are hard to beat. As mentioned earlier, they can easily smash through the rib cage of a whitetail deer. Ideally, you want a significant blood trail, and those large diameter cutting edges produced by expandable blades are going to give you that. Exsanguinate the body cavity of a third of the average whitetail's blood supply (approximately 2¾ pints), and that animal is down for the count, rarely running beyond 50 to 75 yards.

The **Muzzy 100-grain fixed 3-blade crossbow-designated broadhead** has a 13/16-inch cutting diameter, employing its trocar-tip design. Compared to the up-front 'leading-edge' style broadhead, a trocar-tip design proves most effective when it comes to penetrating and blasting bone; hence, Muzzy's catch phrase, "Bad To The Bone." Blade thickness is .020 inch. Referencing **shot #2**, you'll note that the fixed 3-blade Muzzy—"Bad To The Bone" broadhead virtually hit the same hole as the fixed 3-blade Wac 'Em broadhead had.

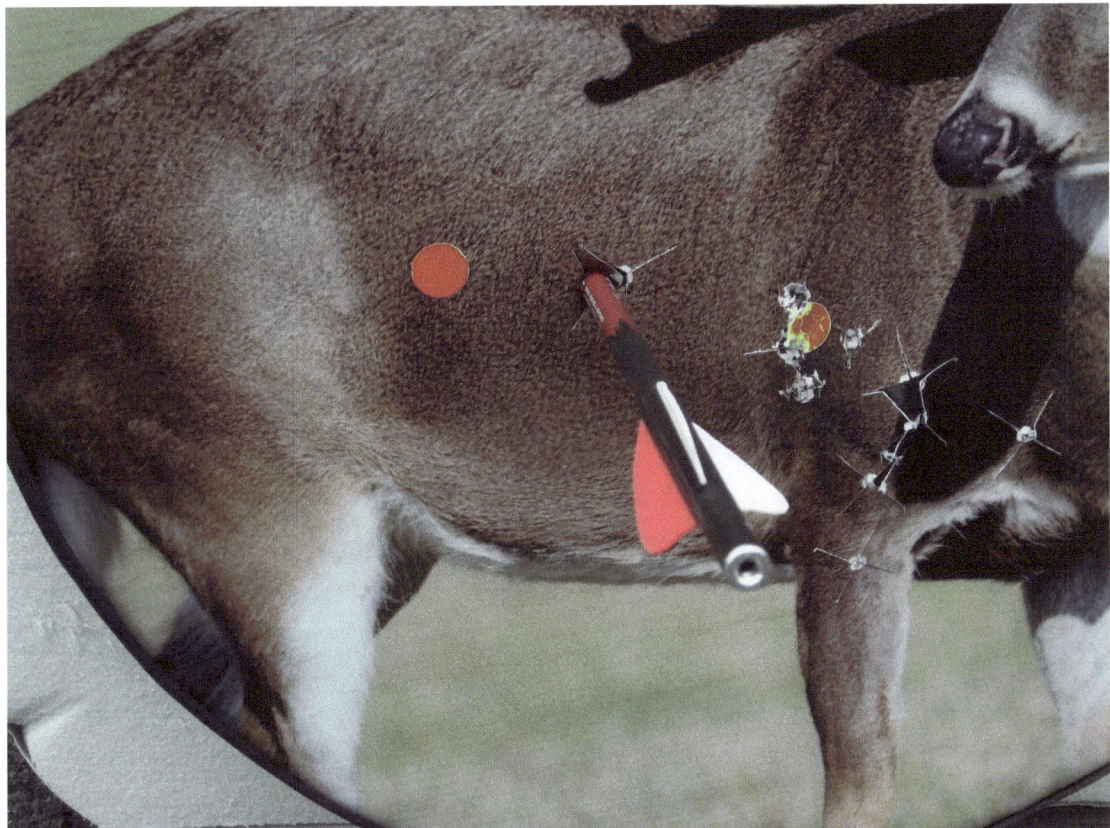

Shot #2 (second group) launching the Muzzy fixed 3-blade broadhead, virtually hitting the same hole as the Wac 'Em fixed 3-blade broadhead

The next and last broadhead we are going to field-test in this second group, before moving on to a third group, is the **Rocky Mountain Warhead X 100-grain 2-blade expandable crossbow-designated broadhead**. It is a reverse 2-blade model with a ¾-inch diameter while in flight, opening on impact to an impressive 1¾-inch cutting diameter. Its stainless steel blade thickness is .035 inch, while its leading edge—cut-on-contact tip—is .039 inch.

After indexing a Rocky Mountain Warhead X crossbow broadhead blade with a cock vane, <u>**shot #3**</u> clearly outperformed both the Wac 'Em fixed 3-blade as well as the Muzzy fixed 3-blade broadheads featured in this group by a considerable margin—one blade of the Rocky Mountain Warhead X striking the edge and cutting into the ½-inch red bull's-eye (indicated by the green exploding flake at the precise point of impact). Penetration was 11 inches.

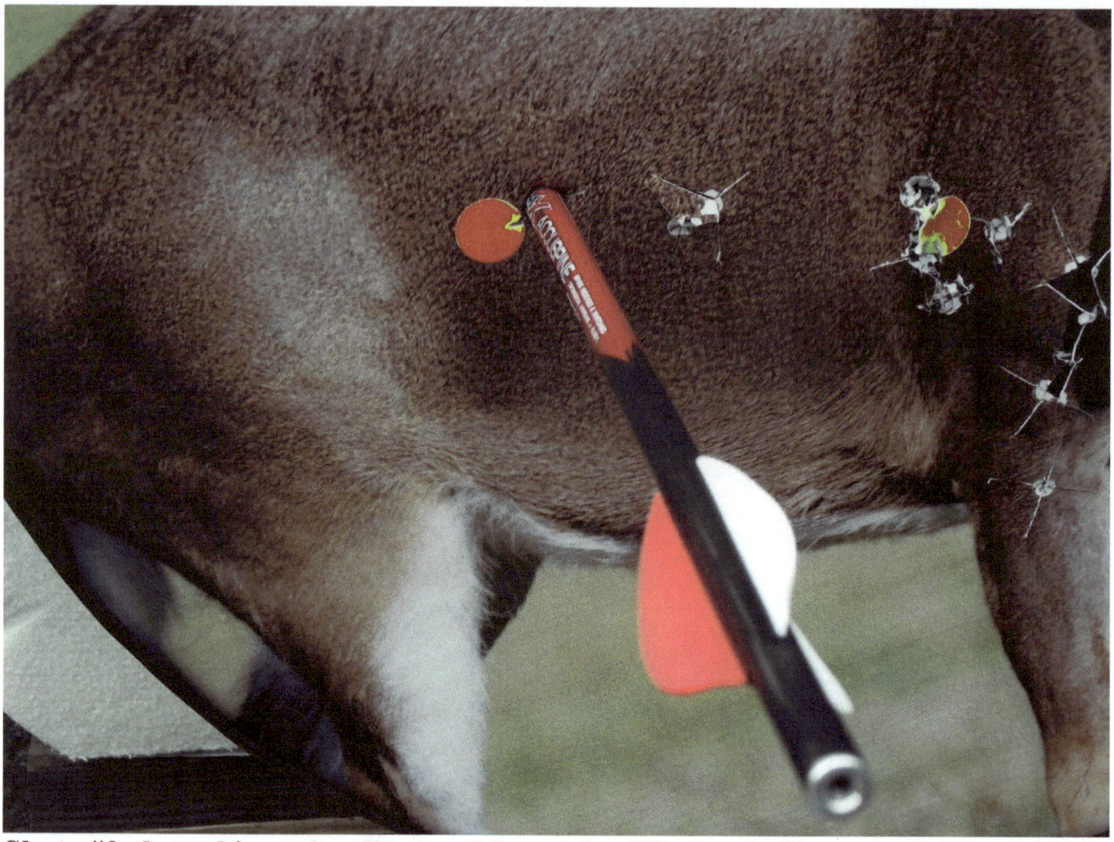

Shot #3 launching the Rocky Mountain Warhead X expandable 2-blade broadhead, slicing the bull's-eye

Let's have a look at the three fixed and four fully deployed expandable 100-grain broadheads that we field-tested thus far.

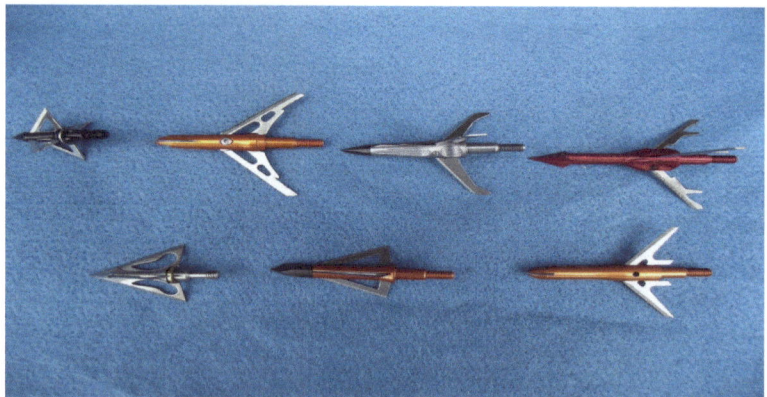

Top row–left to right: Slick Trick fixed 4-blade ~ Rage X expandable 2-blade ~ SpitFire Maxx expandable 3-blade ~ Wac 'Em expandable 3-blade.
Bottom row–left to right: Wac 'Em fixed 3-blade ~ Muzzy fixed 3-blade ~ Rocky Mountain Warhead X expandable 2-blade

After a good many years of shooting traditional bows (long bows and recurves), the more modern (conventional) compound bows, and, more recently, crossbows, I've learned that the way to achieve exemplary field-point accuracy when shooting broadheads is to launch arrows and bolts fixed with plastic vanes boasting a two- to three-degree right helical cant as compared to either offset or straight vanes. Helical vanes spiral the missile much like rifling in a firearm spirals a bullet. One issue is that helical fletching costs more. Consequently, many folks, perhaps unwittingly, settle for "close is close enough" performance and either wind up with straight or offset vanes. The differences are that helical vanes are positioned on the shaft with a slight curve (either to the left or right); offset vanes are straight but offset at an angle; straight vanes are aligned dead ahead, perfectly aligned with the shaft. CAMX Accuspine /Black Eagle bolts are top performers. Although designed for the CAMX X330 crossbow, they should function well with *your* well-tuned crossbow.

Whereas one should experiment with different broadheads in order achieve optimum performance via indexing, regardless of the crossbow employed, it is my strong recommendation to utilize helical formed vanes with bolts as featured by CAMX Accuspine/Black Eagle. Hands-down, these missiles are top performers. As you should initially examine any arrow or bolt, simply whirl the shaft upon an arrow spinner to check for signs of a wobble (even when brand-new and out of the box) then screw in your choice of broadhead and whirl away again, still checking for signs of a wobble. You may be surprised to find that one of your broadheads is out of whack. Incidentally, I've never had an issue with a CAMX Accuspine/Black Eagle bolt. Conversely, I have had issues with broadheads, such as not being consistent referencing grain weights or blades not being properly installed—but never with any of the popular broadhead products covered in these field-tests.

Large size arrow spinner by Apple Archery

I look at it this way. If I can consistently shoot ½-inch to 1-inch groups at 20 and 30 yards, respectively, utilizing field-tipped bolts, I'm going to give myself the added edge and shoot broadheads that offer the closest to field-point precision for hunting whitetails. As we've seen in the first set, the Rage X expandable 2-blade broadhead and the SpitFire Maxx expandable 3-blade broadhead performed remarkably well. The Rocky Mountain Warhead X crossbow broadhead did extremely well in terms of accuracy. Therefore, as mentioned earlier, I'll employ expandable (mechanical) well-tuned (indexed) broadheads for whitetails and fixed-blade broadheads for larger size game such as elk and moose.

Field-testing & indexing third and final group of broadheads

Top row–left to right: Havoc G5 1.5" expandable 2-blade ~ Havoc G5 2" expandable 2-blade ~ Flying Arrow Archery's Orion 3 fixed 3-blade ~ Flying Arrow Archery's Pharmakon (a unique cone-shaped 3-ring pretzel-like blade design) ~ Slick Trick RaptorTrick expandable 2-blade

Bottom row–left to right: Fully deployed Havoc G5 1.5" expandable 2-blade ~ Havoc G5 2" expandable 2-blade ~ Slick Trick RaptorTrick expandable 2-blade

For field-testing a third and final set of broadheads, I set up a new Cube Hybrid American Whitetail Systems target with a fresh graphic of the whitetail deer so as not to clutter up the image.

The **Havoc 1.5 G5 is a 100-grain expandable 2-blade crossbow-designated broadhead** with a 1.5-inch cutting diameter. After properly indexing the Havoc G5 broadhead by aligning one of its blades with the cock vane, <u>shot #1</u> hit ¾ inch to the right of the bull's-eye and ¾ inch low. Penetration ran 9½ inches. As before, experimentation for best alignment performance had been conducted on another target.

Shot #1 ~ G5 Havoc 1.5"

The **Havoc G5 "Terror of Two" is a 100-grain expandable 2-blade crossbow-designated broadhead** with a 2-inch cutting diameter. <u>**Shot #2**</u> hit ¾-inch to the left of the bull's-eye and ¼-inch low. Penetration also ran 9½ inches. You'll note a slightly better result with regard to accuracy.

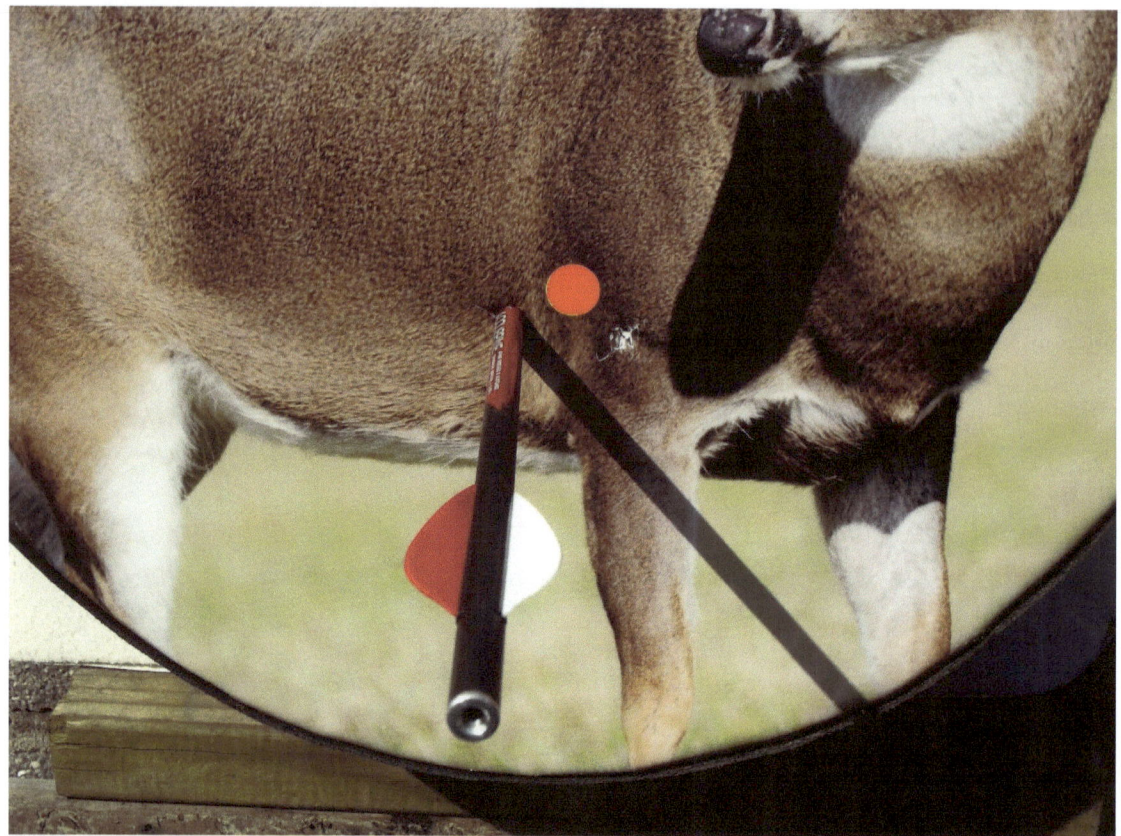

Shot #2 ~ G5 Havoc 2"

Both 100-grain Havoc broadheads are constructed of 100% stainless steel, featuring Lutz blades and employ Dual Trap elastomeric retention-ring collars that are designed for high-speed crossbows.

Note: As a point of information, Lutz blades are made of surgical-grade scalpel quality 100% German stainless steel. Lutz blades are regarded as the "world's finest" by hardcore bowhunters and industry professionals.

Flying Arrow Archery's Orion 100-grain fixed 3-blade broadhead features a low-profile design and has a 1-inch cutting diameter with 1.5 degree offset blades for greater accuracy. The broadhead is constructed of a one-piece solid stainless steel ferrule and tip. The broadhead's chisel tip promises bone-crushing punishment. Blade replacement is available via Orion's interchangeable **Q**uick **C**hange **S**olid **L**ock (QCSL) technology. <u>**Shot #3**</u> struck the same hole as the first shot utilizing the Havoc 1.5 G5; that is, ¾ inch to the right of the bull's-eye as well as ¾ inch low. Penetration ran 9¼ inches.

Shot #3 ~ Flying Arrow Archery's Orion 3

Flying Arrow Archery's Pharmakon 100-grain fixed 3-blade crossbow-designated broadhead is certainly unique. Its truncated cone-shaped 3-ring pretzel-like blade design, referred to as **R**adical **C**ore **D**ecompression (RCD) technology has a 7/8th-inch cutting diameter. Blade replacement is available via Pharmakon's interchangeable **Q**uick **C**hange **S**olid **L**ock (QCSL) technology. <u>**Shot #4**</u> hit 1¼-inches to the right of the bull's-eye and 1½-inches low. Penetration ran 8½ inches. In terms of leaving a significant blood trail, there is little doubt. This broadhead, as its name implies [Pharmakon], simultaneously promises to be the hunter's panacea and the animal's poison.

Nearly completing this field-test, I reemployed the Rage X 2-blade expandable broadhead used in the second group so as to note and confirm consistency. <u>**Shot #5**</u> performed as illustrated earlier; that is, hitting an inch low yet aligned with the bull's-eye—fractionally to the right of center.

Shots #4 & #5 ~ Pharmakon's clover leaf pattern; Rage X 2-blade expandable broadhead

For a wrap-up covering the twelfth and final broadhead, we will closely examine the all-stainless steel **Slick Trick 100-grain RaptorTrick 2-blade expandable**. The broadhead has a 2-inch cutting diameter, featuring Lutz blades. Interestingly, along the ferrule, it has a three-notched setting for the O-ring. The bottom position is for low kinetic energy delivered by bows with draw-weights below 50 pounds. The middle position is for standard kinetic energy delivered by bows with draw-weights above 50 pounds. The top position is for high kinetic energy delivered by bows such as crossbows. Therefore, you're covered quite nicely for long bows, recurves, compounds, and crossbows.

On examining this expandable broadhead, you will immediately note its thin, streamline contour. Blade thickness is .035 inch with a 4-edge bone splitting Trocar-type tip design. Upon impact, both blades open via a patented stainless steel Alcatraz blade-lock pin system. The RaptorTrick broadheads come three to a pack plus a practice broadhead and three extra O-rings.

As it had been several weeks since I last field-tested the eleven broadheads, I launched the same CAMX Accuspine/Black Eagle bolt with a field point into a crossbow-approved Delta McKenzie Speed Bag to check for accuracy. Bull's-eye!

Crossbow approved Delta McKenzie Speed Bag

More on field point and broadhead archery targets will follow in Chapter VI. For now, we'll finish up and see how the 100 grain Slick Trick RaptorTrick performs in comparison to the other eleven broadheads. Back to The Cube Hybrid target designed for broadheads.

I placed a new red Birchwood Casey Shoot·N·C ½-inch stick-on bull's-eyes in the midst of our last group. I removed the field point and screwed in the 2-blade RaptorTrick expandable broadhead, indexed the 2-blade being sure that the O-ring was in its forward notched position. Would this broadhead fly true as had the field point? I set the line of the scope's 20-yard horizontal reticle across the center of the red bull's-eye. There wasn't a whisper of a breeze. I concentrated on my breathing, steadying the fix of the vertical reticle till it formed a perfect cross in the *very* center of the red circle—then squeezed the trigger. Bull's-eye!

A devastating 2-inch cut slashed across the bull's-eye at 11 o'clock as shown. Penetration into the 17-inch tunnel-deep, thick foam hybrid target ran 9½ inches.

Slick Trick RaptorTrick 2-blade expandable. Bull's-eye!

    I attribute the RaptorTrick broadhead's field-point accuracy to its thin streamline body construction along with minimal blade exposure affected by aerodynamics. You'll recall the first broadhead we field-tested, the Slick Trick fixed 4-blade and how it was affected by aerodynamics. Certainly not the case with the Slick Trick RaptorTrick 2-blade expandable. It flew true to form and gave the best performance in terms of spot-on precision.

Slick Trick RaptorTrick 2-blade expandable broadhead removed from archery target

Upon bolt/broadhead removal, just imagine if you will the devastating effect that the 2-inch wide cut would have caused internally after striking the vitals. Note the fully intact blades. Simply insert a new O-ring (included), and you're about ready to head afield.

Tip: After practicing with broadheads dedicated for hunting, I remove it from the bolt and *lightly* sharpen each blade with either an Arkansas stone or a diamond-coated kitchen steel. You might be surprised to learn how even an approved crossbow foam broadhead archery target will begin to dull quality stainless steel broadhead blades. How sharp is sharp? Stretch a thick rubber band 12 inches out from a doorknob then lightly stroke a blade across the band. Did it cut the band? Yes? Good to go. The rubber band may be likened to blood vessels; that is, arteries, veins, et cetera. Once I'm in the bull's-eye—or no more than an inch away—that broadhead is lightly sharpened, inserted back into the indexed bolt or arrow, then set aside for the hunt.

Although the Slick Trick RaptorTrick is clearly the winner in terms of field-point accuracy, the other eleven broadheads that we field-tested are certainly not to be disregarded; we covered their attributes earlier. Together, we've established that expandable (mechanical) broadheads fly truer than fixed blades; and yes, ostensibly three blades are better than two blades, and four blades are seemingly better than three blades, but not at the expense of sheer pinpoint accuracy. Once again, it's all about shot placement. A 2-blade broadhead with a serious cutting diameter and good penetration delivered precisely into the vitals is not going to make that whitetail any less dead than employing more blades. Of course, discussions and arguments will continue addressing any number of concerns, blood trails being at the top of the list.

Knowing where to aim

When I aim at a whitetail referencing a broadside shot from a treestand, I envision the top of the deer's heart for a heart-stopping shot. Note the crease line of the animal's rear front leg, aiming midpoint along that crease and no more than two inches rearward. You'll slice through the lung(s) and heart for a clean kill. Rarely will that deer run more than fifty yards. That's why I strive for field-point accuracy. Hitting further rearward of where I just indicated will result in a liver shot. That deer will eventually die, but you may have a bit of serious tracking on your hands, so avoid that center body shot. A good many folks believe that that's a good shot, allowing for a margin of error: front, back, up, down. That kind of thinking falls into the "close is close enough" concept.

CHAPTER III

IMPORTANT INFORMATION REGARDING CROSSBOWS, BROADHEADS & ARROW SCALES

One of the most important factors to keep firmly in mind is to *never* launch a bolt and broadhead from a crossbow that is less than the manufacturer's recommended grain weight. Therefore, concerning my CAMX X330 crossbow, I'm good to go, shooting 100-grain broadheads coupled to a 310-grain bolt for a total of 410 grains.

Bow speed should, of course, be considered only secondary to accuracy. Achieving spot-on accuracy is awesome! A light 100 grain-weight broadhead fired from a crossbow with a draw weight of 165 pounds (which is what the CAMX X330 exerts) delivers 100.33 foot-pounds of kinetic energy. At 20–30 yard distances, a whitetail becomes harvested history. For larger game such as elk and moose, I'd switch to a solidly built 100 and 125 grain fixed 3-blade broadheads, respectively. Also, I'd both sight in and practice exclusively with those broadheads—as opposed to the expandable type.

Note: Practice broadheads that come as a bonus in some packaging, be they fixed or expandable types, often fly differently than the genuine article; a 'close but no cigar' scenario is usually the case. Both the Rage X and Muzzy packages came with practice heads, which I launched at another target to confirm this comment. So don't be fooled into thinking that a practice broadhead is necessarily going to fly like the real deal.

To summarize the observations drawn to this point via field-testing are that 100-grain broadheads, be they fixed blades or expandable (mechanical) styles, show that vanes (fletchings) positioned *between* broadhead blades do not steer a bolt with the same accuracy as when aligned with a broadhead blade. A helical vane perfectly aligned with a 4- 3- or 2-blade broadhead does fly truer. Four-blade broadheads do not fly as accurately as 3-blade and 2-blade broadheads. Expandable (mechanical) broadheads fly truer than fixed blade broadheads. Indexing (tuning) broadheads properly aligned with helical plastic vanes offers the optimum in accuracy.

Whereas you might select a specific crossbow bolt for hunting based on a manufacturer's criteria that meets your needs, I'd urge you to give indexable CAMX Accuspine/Black Eagle crossbow bolts your undivided attention for unparalleled performance. Fine-tuning your bolts will give you the added edge.

In conclusion, I'll address the chief differences between broadheads designated for crossbows as compared to broadheads designed for vertically-held bows. According to spokespersons representing manufacturers as well as industry professionals, their comments ranged from a vague "not much difference" to a more general "built a bit stronger" reply. However, after communicating with an officer of FeraDyne Outdoors, Jon Syverson, addressing Rage and Muzzy broadheads, he answered my questions specifically. For example, the shock collar on a Rage X crossbow broadhead is designed to have more holding power than one designed for a vertical bow broadhead. Consequently, the Rage X broadhead is built for higher speed crossbows. Too, depending on the manufacturer, a crossbow broadhead may have a larger outside diameter (OD) ferrule than one designed for a compound bow broadhead. For example, both Rage and Muzzy compound bow broadheads have a standard ferrule (OD) of $5/16^{th}$, whereas the standard OD for Rage and Muzzy crossbow broadheads is $22/64^{th}$. Accordingly, the ferrule of the crossbow broadhead is slightly larger in order to extend the diameter of the crossbow bolt, allowing the ferrule to aerodynamically align with the OD of the bolt.

When you do the math and understand the mechanics, you realize how those earlier responses of "not much" and "built a bit stronger" apply. In any event, when either field-testing or hunting with a crossbow, I always opt for a broadhead that is specifically designated for crossbows so as to obtain top performance.

A Consummate Crossbow Hunting Package

It would prove prudent for the newcomer to crossbow hunting to hunt around for a hunting package that combines the elements of a quality crossbow, superior crossbow scope, and precision bolts. In fact, the two companies repeatedly mentioned throughout, CAMX and Black Eagle, have labored together to precisely engineer these components into a unified whole. Of course, there are several other fine crossbow companies around that produce a great product. Do your due diligence and thoroughly research this arena. Again, my preferred choice is the CAMX X330 crossbow.

CAMX X330 Hunting Crossbow Package (four 4-blade Slick Trick broadheads not shown)

The CAMX X330 Hunting Package contains crossbow with ARC 4x32 scope, Realtree camo Side Mount Wishbone quiver upgrade, four CAMX Accuspine/Black Eagle carbon bolts, four 100-grain field points, four Slick Trick crossbow 4-blade broadheads, butt plate extensions plus hardware, Lo-Ready sling, two Allen hex keys, idler roller rope-type cocking aid, wax & lube kit. Compared to the Hunting Package, the Base Package would be shy the Lo-Ready sling, camo quiver upgrade (substituting black in lieu of camo), and Slick Trick X-Bow broadheads. My suggestion would be to select the hunting package because you do want that Lo-Ready sling; more on that in a moment. Too, you would probably want the upgraded Realtree camo Side Mount Wishbone quiver.

Safety is of paramount importance. CAMX's Thumbsaver technology provides unparalleled protection in preventing a shooter's fingers from entering the string path via a pair of auto-return hand-guard shields. Coupled with trigger safety features to avert dry firing, CAMX crossbows are one of the safest crossbows out there.

CAMX's Lo-Ready Sling functions cleverly, if not ingeniously, with CAMX's patented quick-connect/release tabs and button system strategically installed, one button located on the bottom of the crossbow's riser, a two-position button placement along either side of the stock for a truly hands-free or ambidextrous rock-steady aiming/shooting position. A pair of adjustable speed buckles allows you to slide either end of the sling single-handedly and reset its length for a proper fit.

For a comfortable carry position, one end of the sling would attach to the riser, the other to the button located at the far end of the stock. For the Lo-Ready position, you would remove the sling from the riser and attach it to the button closer in on the stock, just below the scope.

I thought about adding a slip-on pad to the sling; however, the crossbow is better supported worn across your body as opposed to hanging off a shoulder. Therefore, a slip-on sling pad isn't at all necessary. Too, if you sling-carry your crossbow and quiver in the inverted position as it should be carried, stirrup approximately between your waist and knee, you have complete control of the bow when maneuvering through brush. While still in the downward carry position, you can immediately swing the bow up for a sudden off-hand shot. Before climbing a treestand, simply shift the bow to the rear of your body. When settled in, with the sling still fitted across your torso, you can remove the front end of the sling from the riser, attach it to the forward button on the stock, and you're in the Lo-Ready position—crossbow and sling never having been removed from around your body. Good to shift about and, once again, with hands-free mobility. There are several configurations referencing sling adjustment. Find what works best for you based on your body build. Actually, when settled in a treestand, I like to remove the sling from across my body, readjust the strap by wrapping it around an upper arm then forearm in military fashion as when supporting and aiming a rifle. In a sitting position, with an elbow placed squarely upon a knee, this is as good as it gets.

It's important that I address the issue of bow speed. The trend today is a move toward faster as well as narrower crossbows. A significant point to bear in mind is that greater speeds put excessive and unnecessary stress on crossbows. Also, radically narrow bow designs adversely affect strings and servings. Many such bows wind up in pro shops for adjustments and/or repair in short order. The kinetic energy delivered by CAMX crossbows (CAMX X330 and the all-new for 2018 A4 model) is all the speed you need to kill any game animal in North America. Speeds of 330 and 370 feet per second, delivering 100.33 and 124 foot-pounds of kinetic energy, respectively, are worthy weapons of mass destruction! Better believe it. Therefore, you will merely be visiting your pro shop or dealer when the time comes for general maintenance—attending to cams, cables, and bowstring—not unexpectedly seeking out a shop for premature tuning or to repair a broken bow.

To further the point, one of the greatest bow hunters of all-time, Fred Bear (1902–1988), killed many animals with a traditional 165–170 pound draw weight recurve bow; among them, grizzly bear, polar bear, tiger, elephant, and Cape buffalo, to name but a few. Fred had achieved five world records. A good many shots were taken in the 40–50 yard range. We're talking some eight-plus decades ago. The crossbows we shoot today are akin to high-powered rifles as compared to the vertically-held bows Fred Bear handled and the arrows he launched. This begs the question of where does one draw the line with a modern crossbow when it comes to speed? The answer is when the integrity of your weapon is being compromised. That's where you draw the line and stop drawing a bowstring.

Of all the big-game animals Fred Bear had hunted, he said, and without hesitation, that "deer are the smartest and most challenging species." In my handbook titled *The North American Small & Big Game Hunting Smart Handbook ~ Bonus Feature: Hunting Africa's & Australia's Most Dangerous Game*, I cover all aspects of hunting whitetail deer, having done so for sixty-plus years. They are, indeed, a savvy, challenging species. Getting up close with a bow is the name of the game.

Correct way to carry a crossbow afield through briers and brambles

Should you not want the Slick Trick XBow broadheads and wish to forego the Lo-Ready Sling, then go with the Basic Package ~ MSRP is $899.99. You could always order the sling separately as an accessory at a later time, which includes mounting hardware ~ $29.99.

Hunting Package ~ MSRP is $999.99.

New for 2018 is the CAMX A4 Crossbow model, featuring inboard cams and axels (via a swing-arm hanger suspension system). The A4 model is whisper quiet. Although the CAMX A4 has far larger cams than the CAMX X330, the new A4 model's outside diameter is 5 inches narrower than the X330 and smartly places those otherwise exposed components within the limbs and, therefore, out of harm's way.

CAMX A4 CROSSBOW

Let's briefly compare the technical specifications of the CAMX X330 crossbow with the new A4 model.

CAMX X330 CROSSBOW	**CAMX A4 CROSSBOW**
Total mass weight 8 lb. 8 oz. (crossbow, scope, quiver, 4 bolts & broadheads)	Total mass weight: 9 lb. (crossbow, scope, quiver, 4 bolts & broadheads)
Bolt: 20 in.	Bolt: 18 in.
Bolt weight: 310 gr.	Bolt weight: 290 gr.
Total bolt weight with broadhead: 410 gr.	Total bolt weight with broadhead: 390 gr.

CAMX X330 CROSSBOW	**CAMX A4 CROSSBOW**
Draw Weight: 165 lbs.	Draw Weight: 180 lbs.
Speed: 330 fps	Speed: 370 fps
Kinetic Energy: 100.33 foot-pounds	Kinetic Energy: 124 foot-pounds
Axle to Axle: 19.5 in.	Axle to Axle: 16 in.
25 in. outside diameter at rest	20 in. outside diameter at rest
22 in. outside diameter cocked	16 in. outside diameter cocked
Power stroke: 12.25 in.	Power stroke: 13 in.
Overall length: 35.5 in.	Overall length: 35 in.
Scope: ARC 4x32 [non-illuminated] Calibrated: 10–70 yds.	Scope: ARC 4x32 [illuminated out to 50 yds.] Calibrated: 10–100 yds.
Base Package: $999.99	Base Package: $1,099.99
Hunt Package: $1,099.99	Hunt Package: $1,199.99
	Expedition Package: $1,299.99

The CAMX A4 Base and Hunt Packages include the same items as that of the CAMX X330 Base and Hunt packages, except that the A4 Side Mount Wishbone quiver comes in camo—referencing <u>all three</u> A4 packages: Base, Hunt, and Expedition Package. Also, the Idler Rope-Cocking aid included with the X330 model is replaced by a Rope-Sled cocking design for the A4 model. This reduces the 180 pound draw-weight pull to 45 pounds with both arms. Otherwise, the CAMX A4 Expedition Package includes the same items as the CAMX X330 Base and Hunt packages, respectively. Additionally, the Expedition Package includes the custom-made soft travel case plus an extra pack of four (4) CAMX Accuspine/Black Eagle 18-inch carbon bolts. Once again, the wizard behind the curtain is David Choma, the design engineer for both fantastic crossbow models.

I find the differences in crossbow scopes referencing the two models rather intriguing. As indicated on the chart, the X330 4x32 scope is non-illuminated, calibrated from 10–70 yards. Interestingly, although the calibrated distance regarding the illuminated A4 model 4x32 crossbow scope is 10–100 yards, only the first 10–50 yard calibrations are illuminated. The 60–100 yard chevroned calibrations are non-illuminated, intended for the purpose of practice—not necessarily hunting unless in the hands of a truly proficient archer. For practice, imagine launching field-point bolts at a 100-yard distance and dropping them into a 3-inch bull's-eye, delivering 124 foot-pounds of kinetic energy!

This would be a good point to briefly mention Winner's Choice bowstrings found on both crossbow models. Simply stated, many professionals consider Winner's Choice as producing the world's finest custom bowstrings—period. Handcrafted quality and laser-measured technology ensure reliability. For those who wish a bit more knowledge regarding string construction, 83% Dyneema and 17% Vectram are the synthetic materials that generally go into building these superior pre-stretched bowstrings. Winner's Choice is brought to you by The Outdoor Group, partnered with CAMX. As your bowstring takes the most abuse in shooting, why wouldn't you want the very best?

On a *Scale* of 1 to 10: Superior Balance Arrow-2000 Digital Scale

A great tool to help aid the archer in achieving field-point accuracy is a professional digital arrow scale such as the Superior Balance Arrow-2000. The electronic precision instrument is accurate to within 0.2 grains. That's pretty impressive. Its dimensions are 5" x 3½" x ¼"; tray size is 3" x 2½" (regardless of advertised item specifications). I ordered the scale from Cabela's ($34.99), which came with calibration weight, arrow holder, and two AAA batteries. The scale has a 2,000 grain capacity and features a backlit LCD display. For many, many years, I had been using an antiquated Lyman's Archer Scale when weighing components referencing compound bows as well as terminal tackle for fishing. However, I wanted precision personified. I wanted every added advantage, especially concerning the rifle-like accuracy delivered by crossbows. The Superior Balance Arrow-2000 Digital Scale offers exactly that. What a joy to work with a precision instrument. On a s*cale* of 1 to 10, I give the Superior Balance Arrow-2000 Digital Scale a solid 10.

Top: CAMX Accuspine/Black Eagle Crossbow Bolts ~ set of four

Foreground—left to right: arrow holder, Superior Balance Arrow-2000 Digital Scale, calibration weight

    The first thing I do after opening a box of bolts, inclusive of 100-grain field points, is to weigh them on the tray of the Superior Balance Arrow-2000 Digital Scale. I list their weights on a sheet of paper, being careful to keep track by then laying each bolt from top to bottom on the table to coincide with my listing. I'm going to open a new box to demonstrate the procedure in a moment.

    The scale has been precalibrated before shipment, but you can verify its accuracy with the calibration weight. Instructions are included in both the manual and on the inside lid of the scale. It was right on the money. The weight of the arrow holder is 147.0 grains, so you would, of course, subtract that amount from the bolt weight shown in the display window. For example, the bolt that came closest to meeting the advertised matched weight of CAMX Crossbow's 20" Premium Arrows (bolts), including 100 grain field points, weighed 556.0 grains, minus 147.0 grains = 409.0 grains. That is ½ grain less than the advertised matched weight of CAMX Crossbow's 20" Premium Arrows when allowing for a +/-0.5 grain weight tolerance. On average, I find a -0.05 to -2.0 grain difference among the several boxes of CAMX Accuspine/Black Eagle crossbow bolts I've carefully weighed. The Superior Balance

Arrow-2000 scale has a default accuracy of 0.2 grains. For the most part, the field points themselves are 100 grains on the money. Those that are off are but off fractionally, averaging no more than -0.02 grains. Remember, in our step-by-step demonstration, I've consistently launched the same bolt into half-inch bull's-eyes at twenty yards. In other field-testing, I've regularly hit one-inch bull's-eyes at 30 yards. All said and done, this is one fine arrow scale, and these are the finest crossbow bolts I've shot to date—easy indexing being the key to their accuracy.

The scale's arrow holder is not only handy for weighing arrows and bolts, it useful for weighing field points separately, which might otherwise roll around and off the tray, too. It is important to follow the manual's instruction when using this precision scale. For example, you want to place an item in the center of the tray, waiting a few seconds before weighing the next item so as to give the unit a chance to stabilize. Again, this is a precision instrument and, therefore, quite sensitive to air currents and vibrations that will affect its reading. I strongly advise using the scale indoors at a normal room temperature and on a perfectly flat surface, away from drafts and other electronic equipment.

CAMX Accuspine/Black Eagle bolt, inclusive of field point, displaying grain weight of 556.0. Subtract weight of arrow holder (147 grains) = 409.0 grain total

Knocking Specific Crossbow Nocks

A final point I'd like to make regarding crossbow bolts is the choice of nocks: Polymer Half-Moon Nocks (synonymous with Polymer Moon Nocks) versus Aluminum Flat Back Caps. The CAMX Accuspine/Black Eagle bolts come with Aluminum Flat Back Caps, but the other half-moon type is available. Here's my thinking on this point. As the nock is the critical connection between your crossbow bolt and bowstring, you do not want a nock that might be even marginally misaligned when coming in contact with the bowstring. A flat back style poses no such issue because the bowstring will always strike the same *flat* surface, unlike the moon-type nock that could potentially strike somewhere between the concave surface if not precisely aligned. Also, a flat back cap allows for removal should the bolt penetrate too deeply into a target as the butt cap is threaded and allows for the bolt's removal via a special tool; the half-moon type does not allow for this. Too, the decision between the two materials, polymer versus aluminum should be a no-brainer. Lastly, as the manufacturer is prepackaging bolts with the aluminum flat back caps already installed, just short of stating their preferred recommendation, why bother with the half-moon type at all? The same holds true for Omni Nocks, Capture Nocks, et al. That's my five-cents worth of input concerning crossbow nocks.

CHAPTER IV

STATING A *CASE* FOR SOFT & HARD CROSSBOW & BOLT CASES ~ EXPANDABLE (MECHANICAL) BROADHEAD CASES

Soft-Sided Cases for Crossbows

For overall protection when storing and/or transporting your crossbow, purchasing a crossbow case is a smart decision. In selecting a case, one has to decide between a hard-shell (plastic) or soft-sided (material) case. Narrowing down this decision is simple. If you are traveling by plane, train, or other such mode of transportation where a bow case is going to get bandied about by baggage handlers, opt for a hard-shell case for ultimate protection. However, if you are in charge of your equipment and not likely to knock the crossbow about carelessly, a soft-sided crossbow case is the ticket.

When Donna and I travel between destinations in our vehicle, be it short distances or covering several hundred miles, my soft-sided crossbow case is packed lastly and rests securely upon luggage and other paraphernalia. When considering either a hard-shell or soft-sided case, a good suggestion would be to purchase a custom-fitted crossbow case rather than a universal style. A quality case that fits your weapon like a glove, specifically made for your crossbow, scope, bolts, et cetera, has definite advantages over "one-size-fits-most" types. Otherwise, always check the bow's overall measurements against the interior dimensions of the case before purchasing.

For example, the five-pocket CAMX Premium Crossbow Case is custom made to accommodate the CAMX X330 crossbow, scope, and accessories. The entire interior of the double-zippered case is padded and lined with a thick, plush protective fabric. Its outer shell is constructed of foam and covered with a heavy-duty water-resistant material. Padded three-point backpack-type panels offer comfort at the shoulders and lower back when transporting the crossbow vertically.

Rear view: CAMX Premium Crossbow Case: wide shoulder and lower-back straps ~ quick-release buckles ~ three-point back padding

A padded, fully adjustable 3¼-inch wide bandoleer-style ambidextrous shoulder strap with side- and quick-release buckles at back give full carry support. Also, the case can be carried horizontally as two sturdy easy-to-reach carrying handles are located on either side of the case. A pair of large slash pockets is for flat items such as topo maps and/or other papers. Two large side-cargo pockets can carry bulky accessories. You'll note that the stirrup protrudes from the case in order to keep dirt and mud out of its interior and is locked securely in place with another quick-release buckle. This is one well thought out, well-made custom crossbow case that will fit either the CAMX X330 crossbow or the new CAMX A4 model.

Interior: CAMX X Premium Crossbow soft case with thick plush padding

A large rectangular double-zipper pocket (approximately 24 inches long x 8 inches wide x 2 inches deep) easily accommodates CAMX's wishbone-shaped quiver with four installed bolts and broadheads, a package of four additional bolts, a spare package of broadheads, relevant instructional material [owner's manual, optional equipment information, et cetera], and with ample room left over for several more items. Also, one could lash the quiver solo to the bow within the case by using Velcro One-Wrap bundling straps, utilizing the large rectangular outer pocket for a protective plastic travel crossbow bolt case, spare package of bolts; more on those items momentarily.

Front view: cargo pockets, slash pockets, large rectangular pocket with Wishbone Quiver and bolts, et cetera

Suffice to say, all five carry-system component compartments vaunt large, heavy-duty zippers with oversized pull-tabs for easy access. Although I wear a waist pack to carry a rope-cocker, scent eliminator container, binoculars, range finder, gloves, face mask, field dressing tools, et cetera, all of these items will easily fit into the two large side cargo pockets. This will give you a good idea of the pockets' roominess. The crossbow case's overall dimensions with bow installed are 34" long x 28" wide x 11" high, tapering to 5" at its foot. The case weighs 2 lbs. 9 oz. Total weight with crossbow, scope, quiver, 4 bolts is 11 lbs. 1 oz.

Don't leave home without a protective case for your crossbow. Aside from doing double-duty as a piece of luggage, it will shield your weapon from dirt, mud, snow, sand, soil, and other grimy materials that can easily find their way into the trigger mechanism, cams, and optics brought forth in an inclement outdoor environment. A crossbow case is a great item in which to not only transport your weapon, especially in a pickup truck or ATV, but to store the bow between hunts as well.

Note: Although the CAMX Wishbone quiver with four (4) installed crossbow bolts fits into the zippered front sleeve-type pocket of the CAMX soft crossbow case (as shown), I prefer to transport quiver and bolts separately; that is, quiver placed within the plush-lined crossbow compartment—bolts (with or without installed broadheads) into an MTM Case-Gard travel case, which also fits neatly into the zippered front pocket. I'll cover that MTM travel crossbow bolt case and others in detail under a separate heading. MSRP for the CAMX soft crossbow case ~ $83.94.

Hard-Shell Cases for Crossbows

Although the catch-phrase for the CAMX X330 crossbow is "Built Like No Other," which is, indeed, true, I still want to protect that investment, especially in situations where the crossbow is going to be shuffled and shifted around say at airport terminals and such. Even if simply shoved about in a cargo area or the trunk of a car, you have peace of mind in knowing that your equipment (crossbow, scope, quiver, bolts, broadheads, et cetera) is well-protected. Plano's SPIRE Crossbow case (model #113200) affords one that kind of security.

The front and rear interior of the crossbow case boasts 1-inch thick, high-density, fully adjustable/removable foam pads (14" x 11¾"), along with 1-inch wide Velcro lashing (bundling) straps to secure and hold both the stock and barrel of the bow firmly in place. I merely removed, measured, and cut two slits in the center of the front foam pad in order to run a strap back through the molded-in plastic slots, over and around the bow's barrel. The quiver rests neatly atop the crossbow's riser. For added stability, I simply lashed a 14-inch strip of ¾-inch wide Velcro brand self-grip strapping material around the barrel and one of the dual arrow grippers of the CAMX Wishbone quiver. You'll note how perfectly its captured bolt with locking knob fits atop the bow's limbs. Four-foot length rolls of lashing material can be found at Walmart for a few dollars—the same material as the 1-inch wide tie-down straps that come with the case and used to secure the stock and barrel of the crossbow. Also, note that the crossbow's inboard-set cams are shielded by a pair of armor tuff, metal limb-tipped caps. It's as if this crossbow case was specifically designed for the CAMX X330.

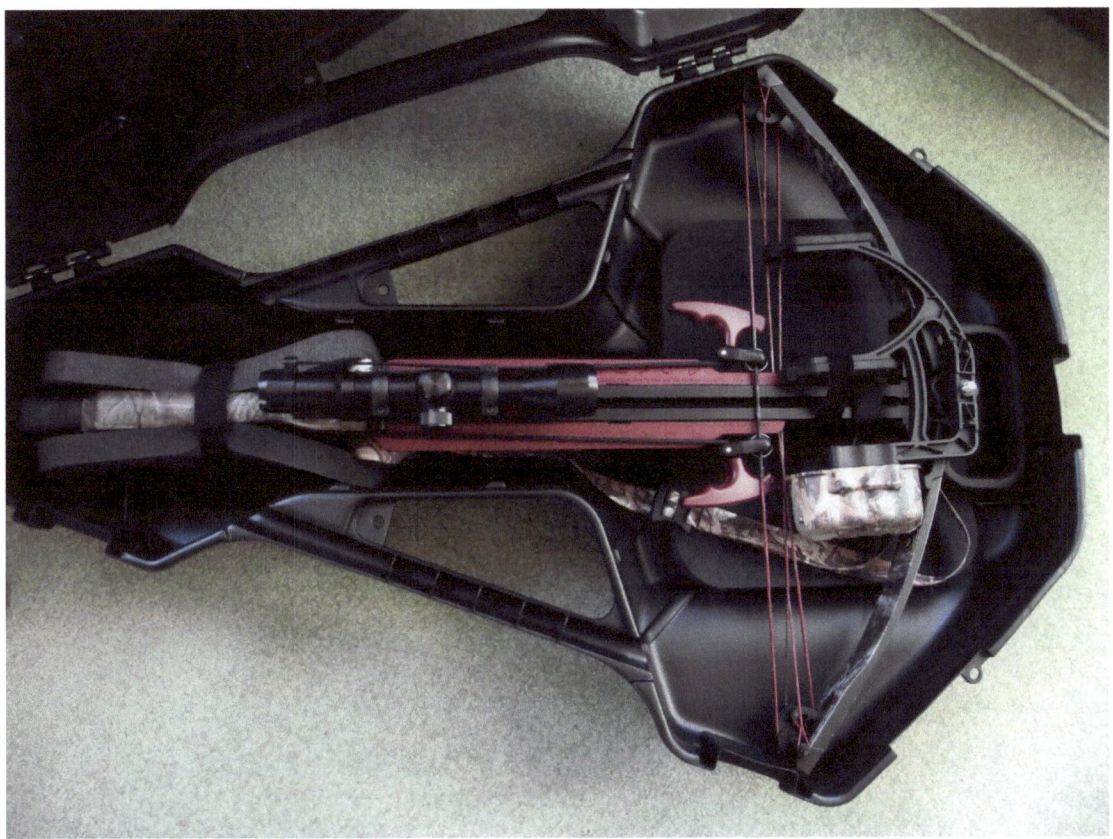

Plano's SPIRE Crossbow case

For well-balanced transport, the exterior of the case features large molded-in carry-handles on each side. Also, the case may be placed upright on its hinged side for convenient storage as opposed to lying flat. Three heavy-duty latches and padlock clasps are provided for secure closure.

Note: The interior of the crossbow case at its widest point is 26 inches, not 27 inches as advertised. The overall width of the CAMX X330 crossbow is 25 inches. Actually, the way in which the bow's limbs are configured into the case left me with ¼-inch clearance at each end—not a half inch—which is fine. The crossbow fits in the case as though it were custom-made. However, rather than rely on a manufacturer's specifications, take your bow into a retail store or pro shop so as to see whether or not it will fit in the case to your satisfaction. Statements made via mail order, such as, "Our compact crossbow cases fit most modern crossbow models," may or may not be the *case* (pun intended). Save yourself unnecessary aggravation. Plano's SPIRE Crossbow case weighs 8 pounds, costing $80–$90. It is money well-spent for the protection offered in a hard-shell crossbow case.

Crossbow Bolt & Broadhead Cases

Plano and MTM Case-Gard archery products are excellent choices for conveniently and safely transporting your arrows, bolts, and broadheads. To keep crossbow bolts and broadheads well-protected, I generally slip an MTM slim-design 24.9" x 4.9" x 2.0" Traveler Crossbow Bolt Case into the zippered front sleeve of CAMX's premium, soft crossbow case; perfect fit. I assemble bolts and broadheads beforehand; for example, fixed blade, expandable (mechanical), and field points for practice. Shown in the foreground is the compact, lightweight yet strong, clear-view windowed crossbow bolt case that holds six (6) crossbow bolts (with or without installed broadheads) secured between two sections of notched-foam padding ~ $19.99.

I carry, separately, the larger black MTM Crossbow Bolt Case that holds twelve (12) back-up bolts. For example, Black Eagle Zombie Slayers, Black Eagle Executioners, and CAMX Accuspine/Black Eagle. The case measures 24" x 5.9" x 3" ~ $28.95.

Both crossbow bolt cases are made from rugged polypropylene and have pin-free hinges with two strong snapping latches.

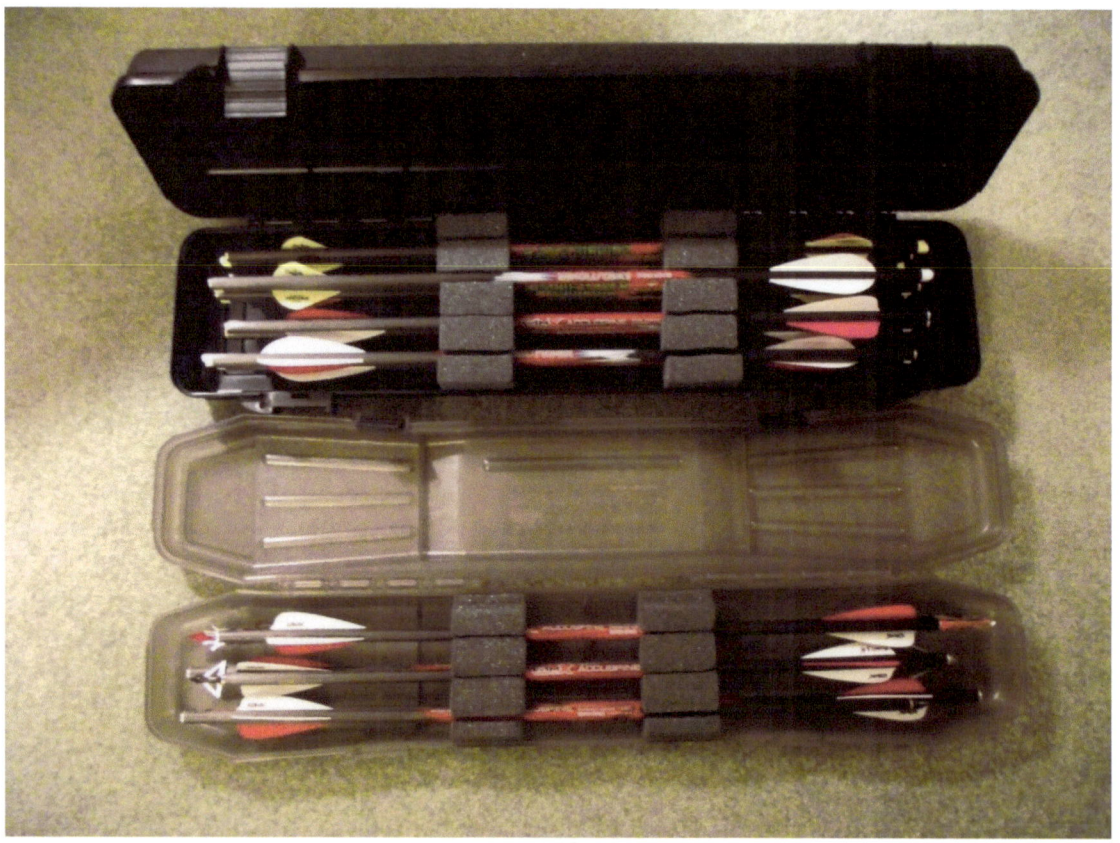

Top: MTM Case-Gard Crossbow Bolt [12] Case.
Bottom: MTM Case-Gard Crossbow Bolt [6] Case

Mechanical (expandable) Broadhead Case

MTM Case-Gard offers the all new pocket-size polypropylene case that compactly, safely, and silently holds six (6) mechanical broadheads sandwiched between a pair of padded foam panels. The Army green case measures 5¼" x 3¾" x 1¼". It is the perfect mini-case for carrying along an extra assortment of expandable broadheads. I keep the wallet-size case on hand in a bow case accessory compartment.

MTM Case-Gard Expandable (mechanical) Broadhead Case

CHAPTER V

STATING A *CASE* FOR HARD & SOFT COMPOUND BOW & ARROW CASES ~ ACCESSORY ARCHERY CASE

Plano's Hard-Shell Compound Bow & Arrow Case

For excellent protection and value in a solidly built bow-guard case for your compound bow, arrows, and ancillary archery items, consider Plano's All-Weather Bow and Arrow [hard] Case. The case conveniently secures your bow, twelve (12) arrows arranged in any combination: field points, fixed blade broadheads, expandable (mechanical) blade broadheads, quiver, release, arrow puller, et cetera.

Plano's Hard-Shell Compound Bow & Arrow Case

The single tool required to organize your Plano hard-shell bow case is a Philips screwdriver. That's it! The case is comprised of a crush-proof Pillar-Lock System, weather-tight Dri-Loc seal, high-density Pluck-Foam padding, twelve (12) rubber arrow holders, and five (5) one-inch wide hook & loop tie-down retaining straps [3 for the bow plus two (2) for accessory items] — all of which are to be strategically placed and secured for the ultimate in customized versatility via many molded-in raised stud-strap bosses. This is one well-thought-out case.

Molded-in raised stud-strap bosses

As one bow's quiver generally varies from another, obviously a quiver mounting bracket is not included with the case. Consequently, Plano directs you to contact the quiver manufacturer for a specific mounting bracket. However, to facilitate quiver instillation, I cut a 10-inch strip of ¾-inch wide Velcro brand self-grip lashing material from a roll purchased at Walmart—the same material as the 1-inch wide tie-down straps used to secure the bow and ancillary items. It is perfect for wrapping several pieces of equipment together, such as tools and other items. I bundle the quiver, arrow puller, release, Husky Allen hex-key set, along with a small pack of spare field points, broadheads, et cetera. In turn, I secure the bundle to the tie-down retaining strap as shown in the upper right-hand lid corner of the bow case, freeing up the secondary tie-down strap (left side of lid) should I need to secure other items.

Bundled up archery items

The interior dimensions of the bow case are 46.5" long x 16" x wide x 6.75" high. Its exterior dimensions are 48" long x 20.75" wide x 7.5" high. The model shown is Plano's AW (**A**ll **W**eather) Series Bow Guard Case #108110. For long-distance travel, I highly recommend this hard, lockable bow case (comes with two keys). At a MSRP of under $100, this is truly a bargain as well as an investment in protection.

Plano's soft-shell Realtree AP Camo compound bow case's interior is constructed of high-density foam padding. Its exterior is fashioned with a "rough and tough" polyester/nylon blend rip-stop fabric. Heavy-duty handles and zippers ensure durability. Item #93375.

Top to bottom: Plano soft-sided Bow & Arrow Case ~ MTM Case-Gard Traveler [12] Arrow Case ~ MTM Case-Gard Compact [24] Arrow Case ~ Mathews Z7 Magnum SoloCam Compound Bow

For light travel, the MTM Case-Gard Traveler [12] Arrow Case will suffice. Either case will easily fit into Plano's double-zippered outer arrow-sleeve pocket.

This soft-shell compound bow and arrow case is one of the best I've come across; however, the item has been discontinued as Plano no longer produces soft-shell bow cases—only hard-shells. Nonetheless, I would go out of my way to locate one if you are in the market for an exceptional soft-sided case. As of this writing, you can find the case online at www.amazon.com ($89.09) and www.ebay.com. Its dimensions are 39" long x 17¾" high x 7" wide with the larger MTM Case-Gard Arrow Case inserted into the arrow sleeve pocket. The large centered outer pocket measures 13½" long x 9½" high x 2" deep. Large, flat net-style zippered pockets run adjacent to the central pocket. Perfect for papers and such.

Archery Accessory Case

Although I have an older model of Plano's Archery Accessory Case, the newer model is basically the same. However, the updated case is a bit bigger, measuring 11½" x 5" x 8½". Both cases have see-through lids, a pair of handy lift-out utility trays with separate compartments of varying lengths and depths, and a foam block inset for assembled fixed and/or expandable (mechanical) broadheads. Within the compartments, I keep an assortment of broadheads and broadhead blades, all labeled for easy identification. In my older model case, the foam block sits deep enough to accommodate broadheads with pre-assembled CAMX Accuspine Loc-n-Load brass inserts, ready for indexing. Either model offers the ease of accessibility to tools and other items. You'll find Plano's Archery Accessory Case the ultimate for storage and taking inventory.

Plano's older model Archery Accessory Case

CHAPTER VI

TARGETING COMPOUND & CROSSBOW APPROVEDTARGETS ~ BUYER BEWARE FIELD POINT & BROADHEAD TARGETS

Videotaped photo from our Cablevision show, *Special Interests with Bob and Donna.* **Donna covers a number of targets used for field-testing.**

Selecting "Crossbow Approved" Targets for field points: Bags ~ Dispatch Target ~ Cube ~ Cube Hybrid/optional inner compression core specifically designed for broadheads

Some manufacturers claim that their targets can sustain field points launched from either type of bow; that is, a vertically-held compound bow as well as a crossbow. As we will soon see, this may not be the case. Generally speaking, most recreational archery targets are designed for bows employing field points—not broadheads. Why? The answer is because a broadhead will destroy a target intended for field points 85–90 per cent sooner than later.

For comparison, as well as to posit an important point, I had launched five Beman field-point carbon arrows shot at 20 yards from my Mathews 50-pound draw weight Z7 Magnum SoloCam compound bow shown resting atop a Rinehart Rhino target bag. Advertised IBO (**I**nternational **B**owhunters **O**rganization) speed for that bow is 330 feet per second. That is in the same ballpark as my CAMX X330 crossbow: 330–332 feet per second. I'm a fairly decent shot with my Mathews compound bow out to 20 yards as indicated by most shots impacted *within* the center black ring of the target. Beyond that distance, my accuracy falls off exponentially as indicated by shots impacted *outside* the black ring. Therefore, when deer hunting with my vertically-held compound bow, I limit my range to 20 yards. I don't need to be tracking a wounded deer for several hours or longer— maybe not recovering the animal at all.

Five Beman ICS BowHunter carbon field-point arrows fired into Rhino Target Bag: Launched from Mathews Z7 Magnum SoloCam compound bow

CAMX X330 Crossbow ~ CAMX Accuspine/Black Eagle Bolts & Quiver ~ Bushnell Range Finder

With my CAMX X330 Crossbow, I'm *deadly* out to 30 yards, having put all four bolts into a 1-inch grouping. Right out of the box, my first shot at 20 yards hit the bull's-eye. I knew that if I didn't first remove each bolt from the bull's-eye, I'd probably be splitting nocks. I didn't want to take subsequent shots at those various smaller targets circling the center because I wanted to precisely note my grouping. Therefore, I launched one bolt at a time, pulled it from the bag then shot another. You'll note my four-shot grouping indicated alongside the single bolt: three shots touching each other, one shot a little low, but all hitting the bull's-eye. A minor adjustment put me in the sweet spot. I back up and record all measurements accurately with both a tape measure and my Bushnell Legend 1200 ARC Range Finder. It always amazes me how accurate that instrument is.

CAMX Accuspine/Black Eagle Bolt ~ fourth shot fired into Rinehart Rhino Target Bag

Twenty shots fired from my CAMX X330 crossbow employing field points at 20 yards were all it took to begin tearing away the center of the bull's-eye. As a comparison, my Mathews 50-pound draw weight Z7 Magnum SoloCam compound bow delivers 102.06 foot-pounds of stored energy; that is, 3.78 fpe (foot-pounds of energy) for each inch of draw length times a 27-inch power stroke. My CAMX X330 crossbow delivers 100.33 foot-pounds of stored energy; that is, 13.3 fpe times a 12.25-inch power stroke. For the sake of argument, both bows delivered approximately the same energy at that 20-yard distance. Why then was the bag tearing up prematurely after only 20 shots? The answer is that the proprietary materials used in the construction of the Rinehart Rhino Target Bag do not handle either missile (arrow or bolt) for very long, especially in terms of constant spot-on punishing accuracy delivered from a scoped crossbow. However, if you were to launch missiles at the surrounding bull's-eyes (eight of them) encompassing the main (center) bull's-eye, the bag would last a bit longer.

Torn up Rinehart Rhino Bag bull's-eye after launching only 20 shots from CAMX X330 crossbow delivering CAMX Accuspine/Black Eagle bolts carrying 100-grain field points

To further the evaluation, let's compare the two missiles; that is, compound bow arrow vs. crossbow bolt. Compared to the Beman ICS BowHunter carbon field-point arrow, the CAMX Accuspine/Black Eagle bolt's diameter is only marginally wider:

Beman ICS (model 400) BowHunter, 31-inch, 417 grain carbon <u>arrow</u> inclusive of 100-grain field point, shaft diameter 0.3125 inch.

CAMX Accuspine/Black Eagle, 20-inch, 410 grain carbon <u>bolt</u> inclusive of 100-grain field point, shaft diameter 0.344 inch.

Therefore, neither the speed of the bows nor the diameter of the projectiles contributed to the bag's early demise so much as the bag's poor construction.

One of the CAMX Accuspine/Black Eagle bolts buried itself deeply into the bag.

To use a bit of hyperbole as well as alliteration, it took a man, a mule, and a machine to remove it. Through the center of the bag, along with the bolt, came a thin, flexible fiberglass-like sheeting material, which the company refers to as their "ballistic nylon dual power-band technology." A representative informed me that it is Kevlar material.

Material pulled through bull's-eye's of Rinehart Rino bag in order to remove bolt

There is no question that the Kevlar material has stopping power. However, even after pulling the sheet from the target, it was *extremely* difficult to remove the bolt from the band. I had to unscrew the field point from the bolt in order to remove it. Although a representative from the company claimed that the bag is approved for both compound bows and crossbows firing field points, this is simply not the case. Nowhere on the target does it indicate "crossbow approved," and that's the important point! The Rinehart Rhino target is best left to handling field points with arrows fired from a compound bow utilizing its entire surface area—not field-tipped bolts launched from a crossbow aimed at the bag's dead center. What the bag certainly does have going for it is its light weight, approximately 27 pounds, which makes it extremely portable. Also, the sublimation fabric printing is superb, molecularly bonded to the cloth, which translates into lasting durability in terms of graphics. Comprising the flip side is a series of twelve circular targets set in a diagonal pattern.

The bag measures 22" long x 22" high x 12" deep and retails from $50 to $60.

Yes, I did address the issue with the powers that be at Rinehart Targets, and they sent me out a replacement bag, but not before my having to direct them to an article I wrote for a crossbow publication covering this matter. Too, they wanted to see a receipt of purchase, which I had on hand from Dick's Sporting Goods. You will note that the new Rinehart Rhino target bag clearly shows that it is, indeed, a crossbow bag: X-BOW 450 FPS, meaning that it can handle the punishment crossbow field-tipped bolts deliver—up to 450 feet per second. Therefore, it can, of course, handle arrows with field points shot from a vertically-held compound bow.

Left to right: Rinehart 18" X-Bow Crossbow Bag for field points ~ Rinehart Pyramid Dispatch/Practice Foam Target for broadheads

The 18" x 18" x 12" bag (item #5711) features two target sides. Twelve 3-inch bull's-eye graphics comprise one side. Five 1-inch and 2-inch crossbow specific MOA (**M**inute **O**f **A**ngle) Grid-Target Sight-in Squares for adjusting your scope comprise the opposite side. The bag is extremely well-constructed, layered from the outside in toward its center with polyester for UV protection, polypropylene wrap for long-term arrow/bolt durability, plastic sheeting for a waterproof barrier, cut foam for easy arrow/bolt removal, and burlap for a superb arrow/bolt stopping core. Also, the bag is truly lightweight, approximately 12½ pounds, making it one of the best portable compound/crossbow approved target bags for field points ~ $49.99. The carry-handle makes for effortless transportability, and heavy-duty grommets at each end of the bag allow for it to be hung.

Although the CAMX X330 crossbow may be uncocked manually via the included CAMX idler roller rope-cocking aid, it is advisable that only adults of average strength apply this method. The best and safest way to uncock the crossbow (any crossbow for that matter) at day's end is to dispatch the bolt into a target such as Rinehart's lightweight, portable, Signature-Series foam Pyramid Target with its easy-carry handle. Like the Rinehart Rhino X-BOW target bag, the Pyramid foam target also has the crossbow specific MOA Grid-Target for sighting-in your crossbow scope. The target stands 14 inches high, 16 inches wide at its base, and weighs 7 pounds. With four bright-white circled shooting sides, this target will last quite some time. MSRP is $69.99.

Field-Point & Broadhead Targets

Let's take a close look at several other "Crossbow Approved" field-point targets. Later, we'll examine the one we used in field-testing broadheads, offering the optional inner compression foam core specifically designed for crossbow broadheads.

New for 2017–18, Morrell's Yellow Jacket YJ-350 field-point target bag is engineered for both compound bows and crossbows. That fact is clearly printed on the bag, informing you that it is a 350 feet per second bag. As my CAMX X330 crossbow fires bolts at a specified 330–332 fps, the YJ-350 fps bag has me covered quite nicely. I have shot scores of bolts into the bag's bull's-eye (opposite side has same graphics) without any sign of deterioration. The target is a solidly constructed framed bag measuring 22" long x 24" high x 14" deep and weighs approximately 35 pounds. The outer cover is coated with a semi self-sealing burlap material. Its inner proprietary properties have superb stopping power and allow for easy one-hand bolt removal. At a price tag under $60, the Morrell Yellow Jacket YJ-350 field-point target bag is a bargain.

Morrell Yellow Jacket YJ-350, rated 350 fps

Need a target bag that can absorb speeds better than 350 feet per second, standing up to the severe punishment from both field-point tipped arrows as well as bolts fired at speeds up to 400 feet per second? Morrell's #1 Eternity Target is the ticket. This 19" x 19" x 19" target can positively take the abuse. It has four graphics at which to shoot: close-up of a deer's vitals, five circular targets encompassing the antlers of a ruminant mammal, dart board, and nine-ball (a variation of pool in which you shoot nine numbered object balls in consecutive order). The nine-ball graphic is clever in that you'll extend the life of the face of this particular side because you are not shooting in one concentrated area but throughout the face of the target. The bag weighs 32 pounds and retails for $77.

In shooting my CAMX X330 crossbow at the Morrell #1 Eternity 400 fps-rated target, I believe the *Eternity* bag will outlast me. The chassis encases a poly-fill, foam, and other proprietary materials. Like the Morrell Yellow Jacket YJ-350 target bag, the Morrell #1 Eternity Target is covered with a coated, semi self-healing burlap. Both the Morrell YJ-350 and #1 Eternity bags are manufactured with durability in mind. They are 100% weatherproof, withstanding the rigors of extreme heat and frigid cold. Rain and snow are not going to faze these targets. Also, the bags' covers are replaceable, so should you ever need a replacement, the material is available. Of course, some disassembly and assembly would be required. If or when that time comes, it would not be a big deal because you can view repair videos on the Internet posted by Morrell as well as fellow do-it-yourselfers. Only after many, many hundreds of shots would this become necessary. Again, you want a target specifically *approved* and fps-*rated* to handle both crossbows and compound bows in the bargain as these products certainly do.

Morrell Eternity #1, rated 400 fps

In terms of affordability, the Delta McKenzie Crossbow Speed Bag will stay the course. It, too, is rated at 400 feet per second, which means, of course, that it will handle field points launched from either a crossbow or compound bow up to that speed. Printed across its upper face in bold letters on both sides of the bag it clearly states Crossbow Speed Bag. Do not confuse the Delta McKenzie Crossbow Speed Bag with its cousin, labeled as the Delta McKenzie Speed Bag—not the Delta McKenzie Crossbow Speed Bag, for the other is rated at only 300 fps and, therefore, not suitable for crossbows. The Delta McKenzie Speed Bag (in green) is shown to the left of the Delta McKenzie Crossbow Speed Bag in the photo beginning this chapter.

The Delta McKenzie Crossbow Speed Bag bag measures 24" long x 24" high x 10" deep. It is not a light bag, weighing in at a hefty 50 pounds. Retailing from $40 to $50, I'd recommend this target bag for budget-minded folks. The consideration is weight versus dollar savings. If weight is not an issue, this is a fine crossbow bag.

Bolt removal is a breeze; better than most. The opposite side of the bag has the same graphic.

20-yard spot-on crossbow accuracy referencing obliterated red stick-on ½-inch bull's-eye via 100-grain field point ~ CAMX Accuspine/Black Eagle bolt ~ Delta McKenzie Crossbow Approved Field-Point Speed Bag, rated 400 fps

Need to exceed 400 feet per second for field point arrows and bolts launched at a target approved for both compound bows and crossbows? Look no further. The American Whitetail Target System's CompCube Bowhunter Hybrid Archery Target, rated for 450 fps is your answer. The cube measures 21" x 21" x 21" and weighs approximately 25 pounds, making it extremely portable. It has four high-definition surfaces at which to shoot: a tom turkey, close-up of a deer's vitals, five 3-inch circular targets plus several smaller ones, and a 14" x 14" graphic of a ten-pointer with exposed vitals. Around the top, bottom, and forward of the buck are six additional 1½-inch circular targets. Bolt removal is a cinch with a one-hand pull. Stopping power is incredible for speeds of up to 450 feet per second. The target retails for $80.

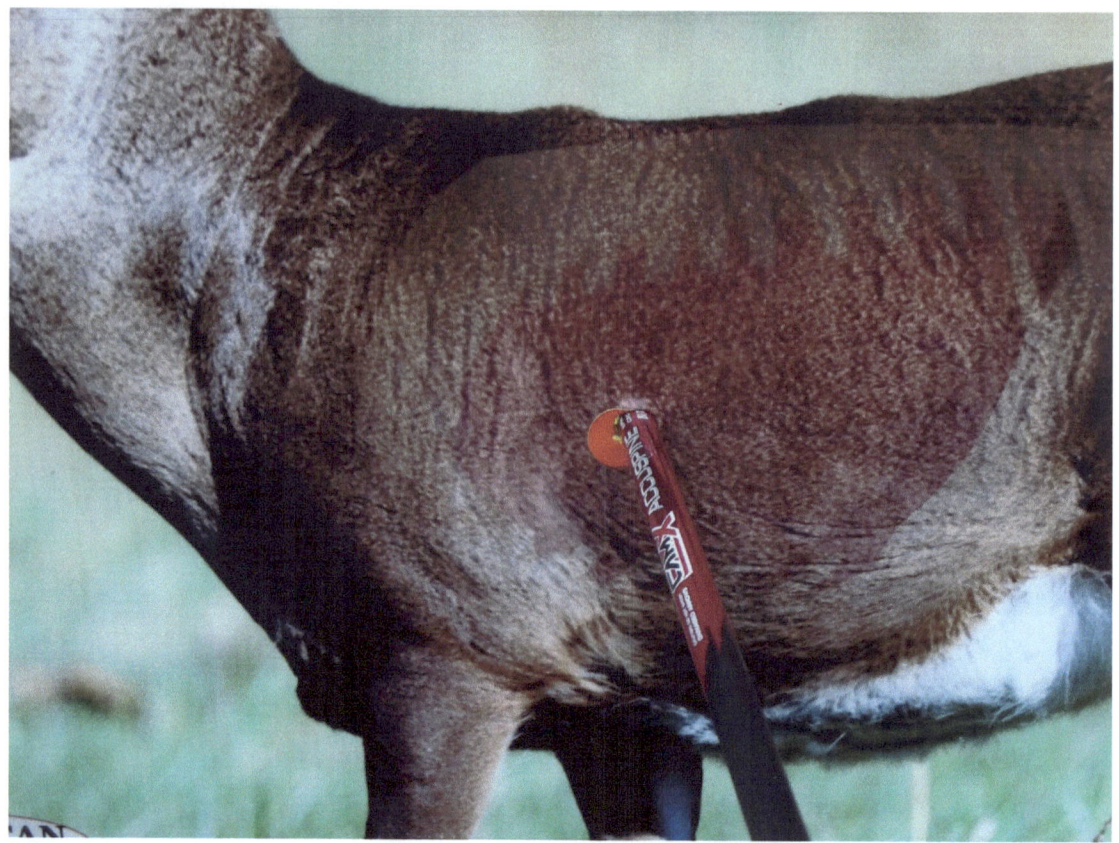

20 yard spot-on crossbow accuracy referencing red stick-on ½-inch bull's-eye via 100-grain field point ~ CAMX Accuspine/Black Eagle bolt ~ American Whitetail Systems CompCube Crossbow Approved Field-Point target, rated 450 fps

Let's now take a close look at a truly unique cube-type target. The Cube Hybrid crossbow-rated target is in a league of its own, also manufactured by the same company; that is, American Whitetail Target Systems. The Cube Hybrid—not to be confused with the CompCube Bowhunter Hybrid—is a professional-grade archery target not only approved for powerful compound bows and crossbows launching field points, it is also approved for broadheads via an *optional* solid-foam cylindrical compression core; more on that in a moment.

The Cube Hybrid is also rated for speeds of 450 feet per second. A bag located within the target's core can be rotated 360 degrees. By rotating the bag after punishing a particular area, then shooting anew, you are in effect self-repairing that area because you have shifted the proprietary material to another section. When you encounter a weak zone after continuous shooting, simply rotate the bag to cover that particular area. The Cube Hybrid measures 20" long x 18" high x 18" deep and weighs approximately 30 pounds.

20 yards spot-on crossbow accuracy at red ½-inch bull's-eye via a 100-grain field point ~ CAMX Accuspine/Black Eagle bolt ~ American Whitetail Systems 'The Cube Hybrid' Crossbow Approved Field-Point target, rated 450 fps

The Cube Hybrid offers extended life—approximately two thousand-plus shots before you would concern yourself with minimal repair. Stopping power, durability, and broadhead conversion are the hallmarks of this exceptional Cube Hybrid crossbow target.

And now for the *pièce de résistance*: <u>The Cube Hybrid with Optional Compression Core for Broadheads</u>. When shooting broadheads (expandable or fixed blades), as we did in our field-testing, you simply remove the bungeed cover from atop the cube, lift out the bag, replacing it with a separate, thick, now 21" deep-foam compression core cylinder. You are ready to shoot broadheads by simply repositioning the cube to face you. You are in effect shooting directionally into what would otherwise be a void, directing the broadhead out of the path of the target's main body. How cool is that? Graphics for the broadhead target may vary between a deer's vitals or a close-up buck. You'll recall that we had launched broadheads at a close-up buck. The Cube Hybrid retails for $109.99; the broadhead compression core retails for $59.99.

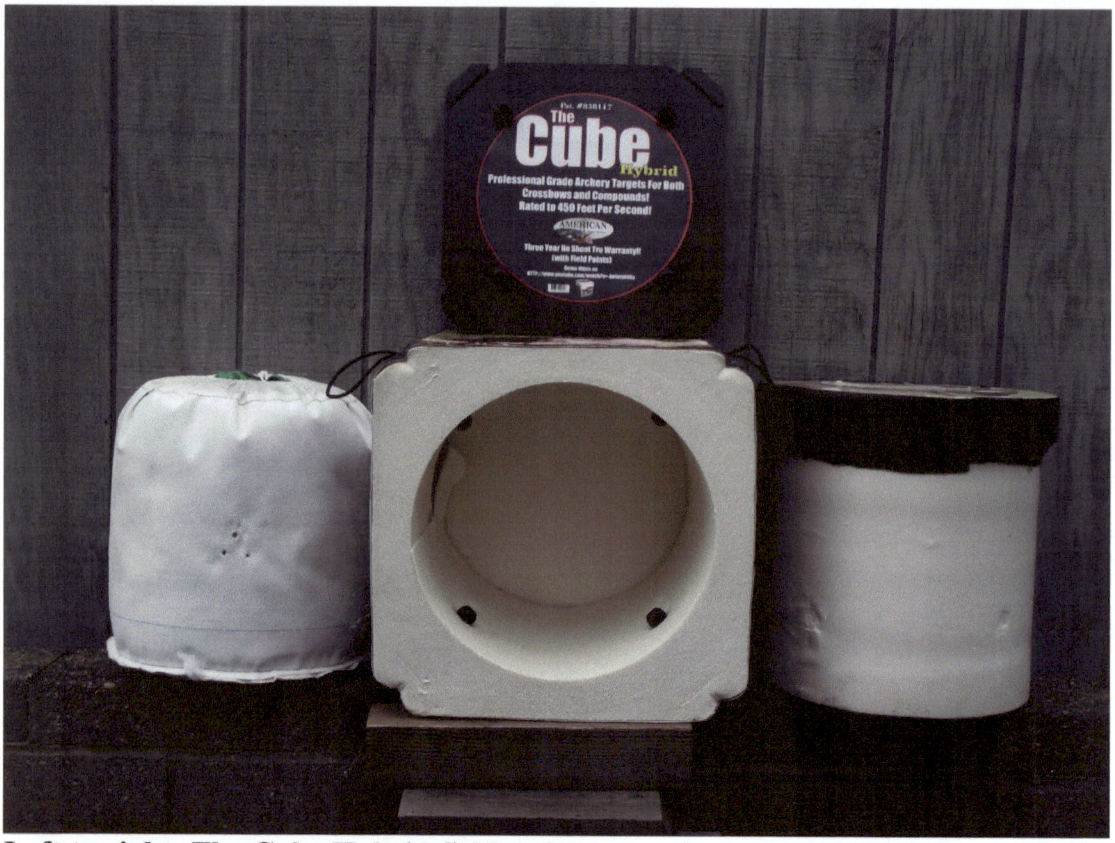

Left to right: The Cube Hybrid field-point bag ~ foam cube and cover ~ optional inner compression foam core with graphic—specifically designed for broadheads

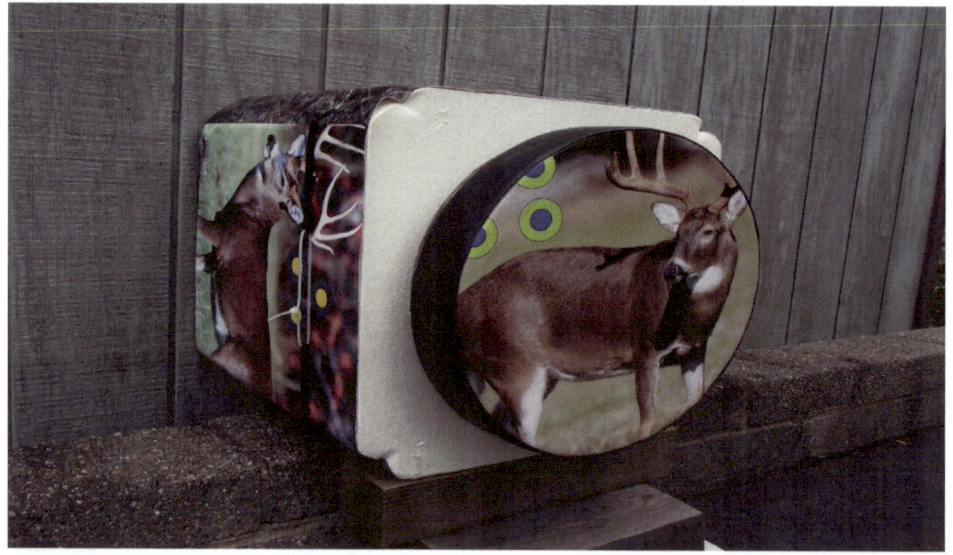

The Cube Hybrid target with optional compression core specifically designed for broadheads

To sum-up, always look for "compound/crossbow/approved" endorsements clearly printed on the targets—not verbally expressed by a company representative or salesperson. Firstly, and most importantly, home in on the rated speed for a particular target. For example, and as stated earlier, a 350 fps crossbow-rated target is going to cover me quite nicely for my CAMX X330 fps crossbow. All things being equal, a rated target speed of 400 or 450 fps is going to offer an even greater advantage in that the target will last considerably longer. Therefore, longevity should be a key factor in selecting a crossbow target. Part and parcel to that decision is buying the best crossbow target that your budget (or your significant other) will allow. In the long run, you'll be very glad that you did.

At the end of a hunt, you could simply discharge the bolt into the Rinehart Pyramid Dispatch Target (shown earlier) for which it is designed. However, what I do first is carefully unscrew the broadhead and screw in a field-point before discharging the weapon. Preparing for the hunt, I only shoot an indexed bolt/broadhead *once* into the bull's-eye of an approved broadhead target so as to keep those blades sharp. Keep firing a broadhead into foam or other proprietary material(s), and you will dull the blades' edges.

CHAPTER VII

SELECTING HUNTING CLOTHING, FOOTWEAR, BOW ACCESSORIES FOR ALL SEASONS

Outerwear: jackets, pants, jumpsuits

The name of the game in selecting hunting clothing and footwear for all seasons is to aim for total comfort. The more time you put into the hunt, the more successful you are going to be. Returning early to your vehicle or lodging because you are too cold, wet, or just plain uncomfortable will, obviously, limit your time afield. Choosing the right garments for the time of year you will be hunting is not only critical to comfort but for blending in with your environment. Picking the wrong camouflage outfit can be as bad as not wearing camo at all. Convincing yourself that one pattern will suffice for all seasons is one big rationalization, for you want to break up your outline as best as possible, especially when still-hunting deer. Unless you are hunting from inside a gun tower, a ground blind, or some such shelter that conceals your presence, proper camo is essential. Even then, without the proper backdrop, camo is essential. I have four basic camo pattern outfits that carry me from early fall through the late winter bow and gunning deer seasons, which also take into account temperature extremes.

For example, a hunting season in Tompkins County, located in the Southern Zone of New York State, had unseasonably warm November/December temperatures ranging from morning lows of 25 degrees Fahrenheit to morning highs of 49 degrees Fahrenheit. That's quite a spread. As virtually all the woods were void of leaves at that point, my clothing selection was a two-piece pants and jacket in a <u>Trebark</u> camo pattern, for my surroundings were essentially a bare-timber backdrop lot. The garment's construction is from Cabela's Whitetail Clothing series. While there are a good number of materials used in constructing quality hunting clothing, keep two fabrics predominantly in mind: Gore-Tex and Thinsulate. The former keeps you dry; the latter keeps you warm. Gore-Tex is a 100% waterproof (as opposed to water repellent), windproof, thin, breathable membrane for all-weather use. You do not want water repellent materials; you want waterproof fabrics. Thinsulate is a synthetic fiber that offers warmth. You will pay more for such garments offering waterproof and state-of-the-art insulating properties; however, you will stay dry and warm. Hence, you will remain comfortable and will, therefore, be able to put in the time needed to have the added edge in virtually any type of weather.

For early bow season (compound bow), I select a Realtree camo pattern.

Everything needed for the following day's hunt is laid out the night before. Organization is a key to a successful hunt.

Early deer season: Mathews Z7 Magnum SoloCam compound bow ~ Realtree camo pattern jacket and pants ~ waist pack ~ light boots and socks

By crossbow season, I'm outfitted for much colder weather. A wool balaclava, hand-warmer muff, long johns, jumpsuit, and serious footwear are keys to staying warm for hours on end in a treestand.

Mid/late fall deer season: CAMX X330 crossbow ~ Mossy Oak camo pattern jumpsuit ~ balaclava ~ waist pack ~ heavy boots and socks

For extremely cold weather, I usually don a one-piece (jumpsuit-style) Cabela's Mossy Oak camo pattern outfit that is composed of darker shades of browns, grays, taupe [brownish gray], and dark green. I generally plant myself 15-plus feet or higher in a big hemlock tree, hidden well within its shadowy limbs and drooping branches. This dual-purpose pattern (for oaks and evergreens) is a must-have garment. As with the Gore-Tex line of clothing, Cabela's also carries their own line of waterproof, windproof, breathable hunting outfits labeled Dry-Plus, which is likewise comprised of a thin, flexible, waterproof, windproof membrane.

For cold, snowy, and/or blizzardy conditions, I opt for Cabela's one-piece (jumpsuit-style) Woodlands Snow-style camo pattern design. Again, look for the trademarks signifying waterproof properties: Gore-Tex or Dry-Plus, along with Thinsulate for added warmth.

For more moderate early-season temperatures, I elect to wear either a camo shirt or an uninsulated light-colored leafy-like brownish-greenish <u>Realtree</u> camo pattern jacket and pants. Hence, there is no need to spring for the added expense of Thinsulate/Gore-Tex garments.

Those are my four basic clothing camo patterns [Realtree, Trebark, Mossy-Oak, Woodlands Snow,] that take me through the hunting seasons for both gunning and bow.

Left to right: safety harness ~ blaze orange vest ~ Realtree camo pattern shirt, jacket/pants ~ Trebark jacket/pants ~ Mossy Oak jumpsuit ~ Woodlands Snow jumpsuit

For safety's sake, I have a three-piece Blaze Orange outfit (jacket, pants, and detachable hood) handy that I wear afield—particularly for hunting upland birds and while still-hunting deer. It, too, is from Cabela's Whitetail Clothing collection. At all other times, I wear an orange vest and hat when walking to and from a hunting location. Although not required in New York State, I strongly suggest adopting this prudent procedure. Some private hunting clubs do make this their rule, requiring a certain percentage of Hunter Orange material to be displayed upon your person via jacket, hat, et cetera. Know the hunting regulations in your state before venturing out.

Additionally, I have two uninsulated hooded outer-shell camo garments to wear over my Blaze Orange jacket, pants, and hood when needed. Pictured from left to right is a 10X (brand name) Gore-Tex hooded rainwear outfit (dark-colored Realtree camo pattern); Cabela's Blaze Orange outfit; and a long, oversized, inexpensive Cabela's polyester hooded (light-colored Realtree camo pattern) outfit, which can completely cover the Blaze Orange garment in a nanosecond.

Rainwear in dark Realtree camo, Blaze Orange, light Realtree camo

Also, I carry a green, lightweight hooded rain poncho within a pouch of a seven-pocket Realtree camo pattern RedHead (brand name) Waist Pack. I have the pack set up strictly for bowhunting, carrying only the essentials I need as pictured.

Bowhunting Waist Pack & Paraphernalia

Sweeping from top left to right then down: camo Mini Maglite (attached to waist pack), field-dressing gloves, ChapStick, small roll of orange or red trail-ribbon tape, poncho, archer's Allen hex key set, hand and toe warmers, knife (very sharp), compact binoculars (8 x 12mm), orange haul strap, camo handkerchief, haul line, gloves, headlamp, compass, bow/pack hook, neck gaiter, and see-through face mask.

Last but not least, a hunting wardrobe would not be complete without balaclavas (headgear exposing only part of the face) in the aforementioned camo patterns. For cold-weather hunting, I like the hat-type balaclava, which can be quickly converted to cover both head and most of your face. Not only does it protect you from the elements, it breaks up your facial outline. I cannot stress enough the importance of this often-overlooked item. Both the skin of your face and hands can be dead giveaways to a wary whitetail. Shooting gloves or mittens will take care of the latter; a balaclava will hide your telltale features. Skin will give off a glimmer in certain lighting regardless of ethnicity. Although fully camouflaged except for my face on two occasions, I have been made by cautious deer. I am convinced in the second encounter that the suspicious animal clearly distinguished my facial features apart from the rest of my melded form. I sat unblinking, staring down from my perch; it stood looking up fixedly. I knew he knew. That was the last time I ever let that happen. Even in uncomfortably warm weather, I wear screen-like, breathable face covering—leaving nothing to chance.

In a moment I'll cover an indispensable item worth considering for both bow as well as gun hunting, but first a word about caring for your apparel and accessory items is definitely in order because this is often an overlooked area. You do not want to ruin an outfit that has cost you hundreds of dollars. Instructions are generally noted on the backside of the label; that is, behind the tag that describes the garment's construction. Such important instructions as how to *wash* your outfit are succinct and specific. It may state do's and don'ts such as to Machine Wash in Cold Water–Delicate Cycle; Hand Wash Only and Line Dry; Air or Tumble Dry Low and Remove Promptly; Powder Detergent Only; No Bleach; Do Not Dry Clean, Steam, Iron, or Press; Zip Zippers and Snap Buttons, et cetera. After several washings, you may not be able to read these instructions. Therefore, I suggest taking a moment to record and file this data. These expensive outfits may be constructed of a combination of shells and linings and insulation comprised of Gore-Tex, cotton, polyester, neoprene (synthetic rubber), nylon, olefin, Thinsulate, ad infinitum. Most of these outfits can be washed with a liquid detergent such as Arm & Hammer, labeled "Free of Perfumes and Dyes." Whether using a powder or liquid detergent, a scent-free washing medium is a must, for a deer's nose is its most powerful defense. Do not delude yourself in this respect, for even in a treestand high above the animal's line of scent, a downdraft could give you away in a heartbeat. Again, give yourself this imperative added edge.

Undergarments

Insulated base-layer clothing is the key to keeping warm in woods, fields, and mountains while hunting. Knowing the ambient temperature in the area you are going to be pursuing game will help you determine the clothing needed for a comfortable hunt. I have sets in various thicknesses (lightweight, mid-weight, and heavyweight). I have had undergarments comprised of blended materials such as cotton, wool, nylon, silk, poly-fleece, et cetera. The important thing is that the base-layer material next to your skin wicks moisture away via capillary action, not trap moisture, which will make you feel cold.

Undergarments designed with these wicking properties in mind help to evaporate moisture through that base-layer material and retain body heat. Whether you are selecting a one-piece undergarment (union suit), two-piece undergarment ~ top and bottom (long johns), single- or double-layered material(s), thermal or however labeled, the rule of thumb is that synthetic materials accomplish this better than natural fibers. Then again, natural fibers help keep you warm. Hence, the world of blended synthetic fabrics and natural fibers enter the picture. Yes, life is, indeed, a compromise. To *help* narrow your selection, consider the degree of activity. For instance, while deer hunting, I spend most of my time sitting or standing in a treestand. Therefore, I am not exerting myself to the point of perspiring. Ostensibly, and strictly speaking, I'd be considering wool over polyester. Wool, especially Merino wool, is a wise choice because it is an extremely warm natural material—to the exclusion of goose down being bulky and impractical. On the flip side is polyester, undoubtedly one of the wicking-*est* of synthetic properties, but it doesn't breathe. Cotton does. What to do.

One of my cold-weather selections for the above application is a union suit composing two layers: an outer layer blend comprised of 50% cotton, 40% wool, 10% nylon, and an inner layer of 100% cotton. I love this undergarment for hunting; it is manufactured by Duofold. Additionally, two companies that I would seriously consider for quality top and bottom undergarments are Carhartt and Under Armour. For a comfortable fit, I find that Under Armour's sizing system tends to run small, so I go up one size when ordering. Their base-layer insulating system is offered in ratings ranging from material thicknesses of 1.0–4.0. As there are many variables to consider in selecting undergarments to fit *your* needs, do a bit of research concerning these three companies. Again, always read the manufacturer's Care/Content information label.

A less expensive alternative for base layering is Cabela's 100% polypropylene undergarments. Hunt around and you're sure to find bargain pricing. My Cabela's three-piece top, bottom, and hood (head sock), has been washed many, many times over the course of years. I also have a set of Under Armour's 2.0 Base, long johns, along with my beloved one-piece Duofold union suit.

Footwear: socks, sock liners, and boots

Depending on the weather, terrain, and especially your hunting application, select socks, sock liners, and boots according to their materials and type of construction.

With regard to socks and sock liners, select quality footwear from such manufacturers as Wigwam Mills and REI (**R**ecreational **E**quipment **I**ncorporated).

Google Wigwam's and REI's fine assortment of Merino wool hiker and boot socks. For example, a good blend of materials that go into a pair of Wigwam's Merino wool hiker socks are Merino wool (67%), nylon (21%) elastic (7%), acrylic (5%). Interestingly, their Canada model crew sock—Wigwam's thickest and warmest pair—is comprised of traditional wool (48%) [not Merino wool], acrylic (25%), nylon (17%), olefin (10%). Carefully reading fabric labels gives you a sense of these insulating and ancillary properties. A cushioned sole versus all-around cushioning comfort is another consideration that these two Wigwam models offer.

REI-brand Merino Wool Expedition Socks are constructed from merino lamb's wool, nylon, and Lycra (a brand of spandex) for elasticity. They are a heavyweight, cushioned, cold-weather classic. Coupled with a pair of Silk One Liner Socks, you're good to go in total comfort. Sitting and/or standing in a treestand for hours on end, you will come to appreciate these socks.

Additionally, socks and sock liners from Cabela's have served me well over the years, and you will find some good bargains from time to time. However, I feel that the aforementioned brands are a notch or two up from others. You pretty much get what you pay for when it comes to these items—hunting apparel notwithstanding.

Boots

When it comes to hunting boots, I suggest not hunting around for a bargain. Selections of hunting boots abound, but only two manufacturers satisfy my expectations. Over the years, I've narrowed the list down to two companies: Sorel and the Original Muck Boot Company. Both these boots serve different applications.

For serious cold-winter weather hunting boots, Sorel is a name that stands out among the best of the best. Originating in Kitchener, Ontario in 1962, the company was acquired by Columbia Sportswear Company in 2000, which is now located in Cedar Mill, Oregon. My pair of Sorel Men's model 1964 Premium T-style Boots is a seam-sealed, rubber lower, leather upper, 100% waterproof winner. Within the boot is a removable thick felt liner and insert that helps keep my feet warm and comfortable during those endless hours in a treestand. Combined with a pair of REI-brand Merino Wool Expedition Socks, along with a pair of Silk One Liner Socks previously mentioned, you will come to appreciate this trio's warmth and comfort. Rarely, do I even find the need to slip in a pair of toe warmers.

For more ambulatory movement, trekking through muck and mire, I wear The Original Muck Boot Company's over-the-calf Woody Max Cold-Conditions Hunting boot. This 100% waterproof, lighter premium 17¼-inch tall quality boot is constructed with a 9½-inch-high front and rear rubber bottom with scalloped 7¾-inch-high rubber sides. The upper outer section has a nylon Mossy Oak camo pattern; the inner portion is comprised of a fleece lining, nylon jersey material, and 2mm of thermal foam underlay added to the instep for additional warmth.

Laser Rangefinders

A laser rangefinder is an invaluable tool for those who concern themselves with pinpoint accuracy in lieu of a "close is close enough concept," especially when launching an arrow or bolt from a treestand. An example of this is when I practice from the ground before moving to an elevated position such as a treestand or the balcony of my son's cabin. My Bushnell Legend 1200 ARC laser rangefinder or Nikon Arrow ID (**I**ncline/**D**ecline) 3000 laser rangefinder calculates *line of sight* from perch to target, *degree of angle*, and instantly compensates for *true distance* measured in yards. Knowing actual distance, you then simply align the proper sight-pin of your compound bow or the crosshairs of your crossbow scope on target for that *true distance* measurement.

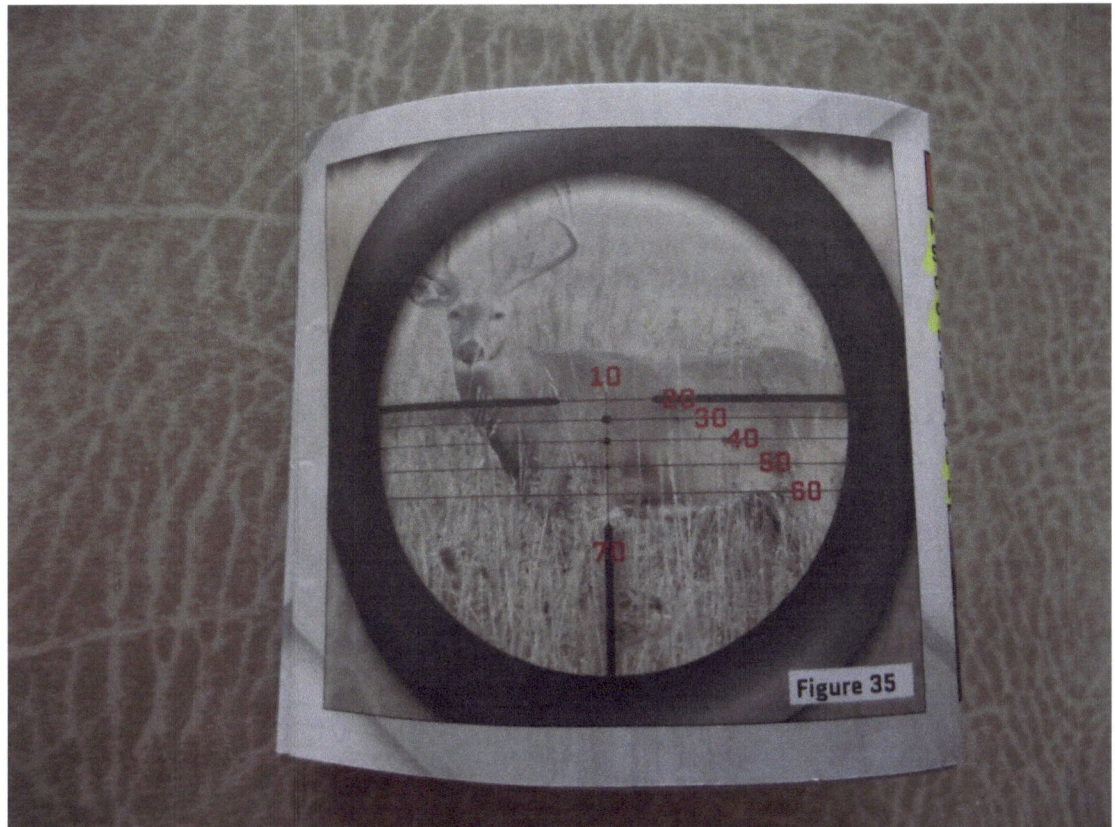

Looking through the CAMX 4x32 ARC crossbow scope — photographed from manual

Distances of 20 yards and elevations of approximately 15 to 20 feet may only require a 1 yard crossbow scope adjustment and seem negligible at first blush to some folks. Hence, let's take another bow-mode example where distances become exponentially greater. For instance: You are in a treestand at a guesstimated height (not important). You are setup with a view of a narrow egress corridor where you expect a deer might appear. Your guesstimated range is 30 yards away. Not a bad guess, guy, but let's now eliminate the guesswork. You take a reading with a laser rangefinder. The instrument reads a *32 yard line of sight* from where you anticipate a nice buck to appear. The readout will show a *-44° angle* (not important). What *is* important is that the readout will also show a *"true distance"* of 23 yards, not a *32 yard line of sight* picture. Had you launched an arrow, figuring that the deer was 32 yards away, you would have shot over the top of the animal because of the sharp angle.

Got the picture? Good. Give yourself the added edge and purchase a quality rangefinder. It's a wise investment.

**Top: Bushnell case and Legend 1200 ARC laser rangefinder (see Author's Note)
Bottom: Nikon Arrow ID 3000 laser rangefinder in its own case.**

The Bushnell Legend 1200 ARC Rangefinder offers both gun and bow operating modes. The Nikon Arrow ID 3000 Rangefinder is dedicated to bowhunting. Both instruments are compact and lightweight. I carry the Bushnell rangefinder in my fanny pack for gunning, the Nikon rangefinder in my waist pack for bowhunting. I wouldn't go afield without one or the other. As this handbook is geared to bowhunting, you need not concern yourself with the discontinued Bushnell Legend 1200 ARC Rangefinder. I mention it and a suggested replacement for those who both gun and bow hunt and need both operating modes in a single instrument. Otherwise you are good to go with the Nikon unit.

Trail Camera

On a final note, another invaluable tool for the hunter is a good trail camera. I say *good* because there are a good number of poor choices from which to select; poor in terms of quality; poor with regard to price. You can spend a lot for a trail camera for features you may not need. As the thrust of my work and play is to keep things simple, paradoxically I work hard in terms of research and field-testing in order to fill a certain niche—ironically, simplicity personified. The Bushnell 16MP Trophy Cam

High Definition Essential E3 Trail Camera is a basic "good as it gets" instrument that will give you an added edge in pursuit of game.

For openers, the camera boasts a true one year battery life, a fast trigger speed of 0.3 seconds; day/night auto sensor for 24 hour operation; infrared 32 LED night vision flash for covert coverage; high-resolution full-color daytime images [black & white evening]; date, time and temperature stamped on every image . . . and the list goes on. The instruction manual for setup is *easy* to follow, and the camera is *simple* to use. Once again, give yourself the added advantage of knowing what's going on in your neck of the woods while you're fast asleep or away from the area for a period of time. You'll be amazed at what you will see and learn.

CHAPTER VIII

BOWFISHING ON A BUDGET: FOR BEGINNERS & BEYOND

Bows & Draw Weights

After many years as a fisherman and hunter, I had bowfishing on the brain and on my bucket list. I thought why not combine the two sports, fishing and hunting? I have maintained the tradition of hunting white-tailed deer with a slug gun while growing up in New Jersey, later on Long Island as well as Central New York. I have also hunted whitetails with a compound bow for many a moon, most recently with a handgun. Of course, and covered earlier, I have my sights lined up for hunting for both small and big game with a crossbow. During last spring/summer interim, I've delved into bowfishing, which can prove rather frustrating for folks new to the game, not only in terms of the hunt, but in selecting gear as well. Referencing equipment, it was an easy and inexpensive transition for me because I had a couple of vintage Stemmler 45–60 draw weight compound bows collecting dust from days of old. Realizing that compound bows, both old and new, are predrilled to accept virtually any type of bowfishing reel, it seemed the natural way to proceed, and initially I did just that.

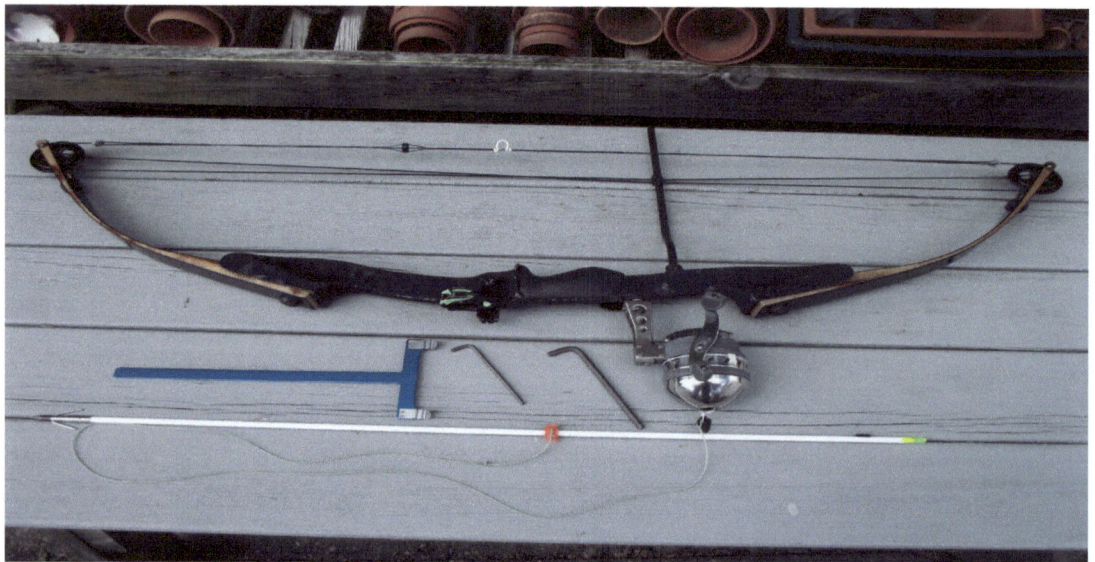

A vintage Stemmler <u>compound bow</u> initially used for deer hunting, converted to a bowfishing setup: Muzzy Mantis arrow rest ~ Muzzy bracketed model #1069 XD Pro bowfishing spin-style reel ~ Muzzy Classic Bowfishing Arrow with AMS safety slide ~ simple Allen hex key tools for conversion

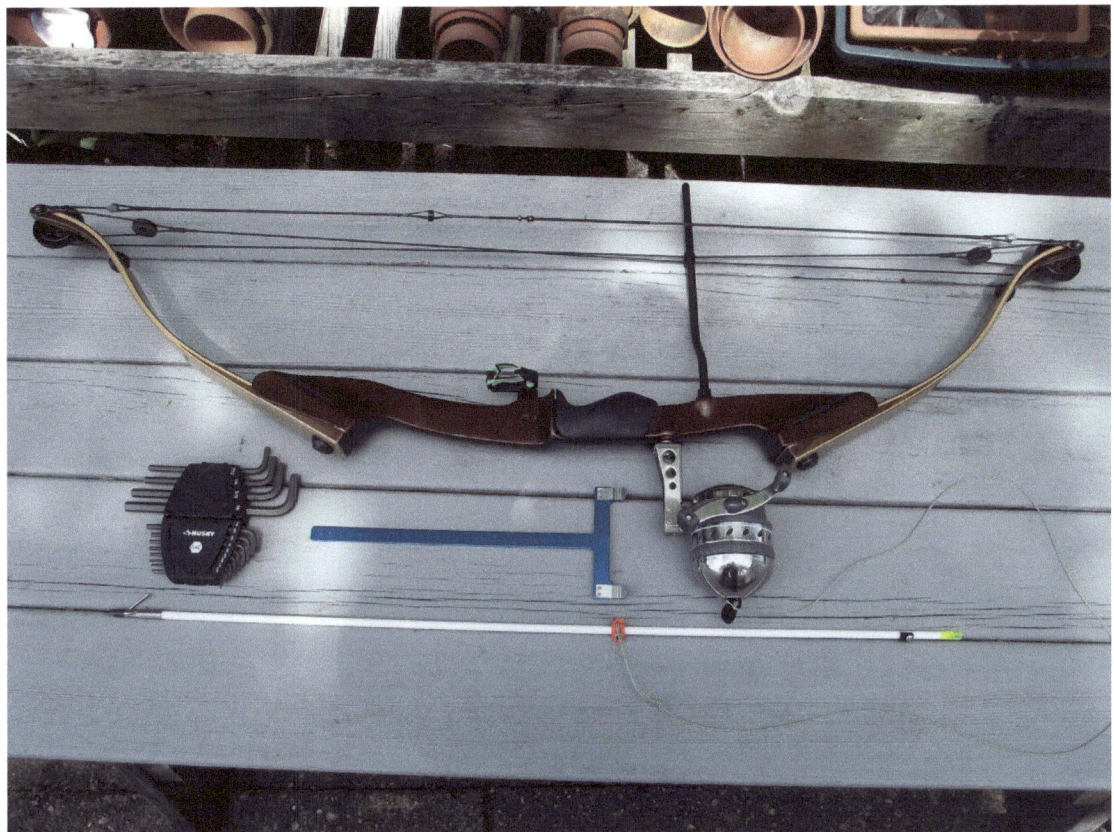

A vintage Stemmler <u>compound/recurve bow</u> also initially used for deer hunting, converted to a bowfishing setup: Muzzy Mantis arrow rest ~ Muzzy bracketed model #1069 XD Pro bowfishing spin-style reel ~ Muzzy Classic Bowfishing Arrow with AMS safety slide ~ simple Allen hex key tools for conversion

First a bit of background information in addition to savvy advice regarding draw weights as they pertain to bowfishing in general. You do not need a 60–70 pound draw weight bow to impale a carp, which is the species that we are limited to legally shoot in our local New York State waters. A 40-pound draw weight would be perfect. Back in the day, I could easily handle a 70-pound draw weight compound bow for deer hunting, so I ultimately upgraded from those 45–60 Stemmlers to a more modern Mathews 70-pound draw weight SoloCam compound bow before eventually downsizing to a much lighter Mathews 50-pound draw weight Z7 Magnum SoloCam compound bow because age was creeping up on me.

Regarding those dated yet venerable Stemmler compound bows, they would prove sufficient for bowfishing because I could back the draw weight off 10–15 pounds if needed. Both bows worked well. But compound bows, with their cams and wheels, become messy as they tend to collect mud, blood, fish guts, vegetation and such. I thought about and thoroughly researched traditional recurve bows designed specifically for bowfishing. No cams and/or wheels to act like a magnet for collecting a mess. Keep in mind that a good many traditional recurve bows do not have predrilled inserts (bushings) installed to accommodate bow-reel seats or integrated bow-reel brackets. Hence, a specifically designed bow for bowfishing would be the answer. But what bow and what reel(s) would serve my needs? I wanted to keep things simple, so as always, I took the simple route—simple as well as inexpensive. I had done my homework.

Unless you are going after gators, or aquatic game with scales the size of arapaima (world's largest freshwater fish), the Muzzy Addict takedown recurve bowfishing setup is the best bet for a beginner. As a matter of fact, it will serve admirably as your mainstay weapon for both fresh water and salt water as I target practice on a partially submerged plastic container in the suds. I leave my takedown bow permanently set up, meaning its limbs and reel remain attached to the riser; I string the bow at a moment's notice.

While we're at this juncture, I'd like to point out that stringing a recurve bow without the aid of a bow stringer is not wise, especially when you get up into the 40-pound-plus draw weight category. Why? The answer is because you will be putting undue stress on the limbs in the wrong direction, and they will eventually warp over time from twisting when using the step-through method of stringing a bow, particularly those limbs and tips comprised of wood material. Also, employing the push-pull method with a bow of a heavier draw weight requires a good deal of strength to put the limbs under tension. Too, the position of the limb's tip against your foot, near or on the ground, invites trouble. Slip and you've at the very least marred the tip. In a hurry to string their bows, I have witnessed folks smack themselves in the head or damage a limb tip. A bow stringer is easy to use and the safest way to string and unstring your bow. One of the best stringers I found is the new adjustable limb-saver recurve bow stringer from Selway Archery, Inc. Easy to use and comes with simple instructions. Cheap insurance for around $12.

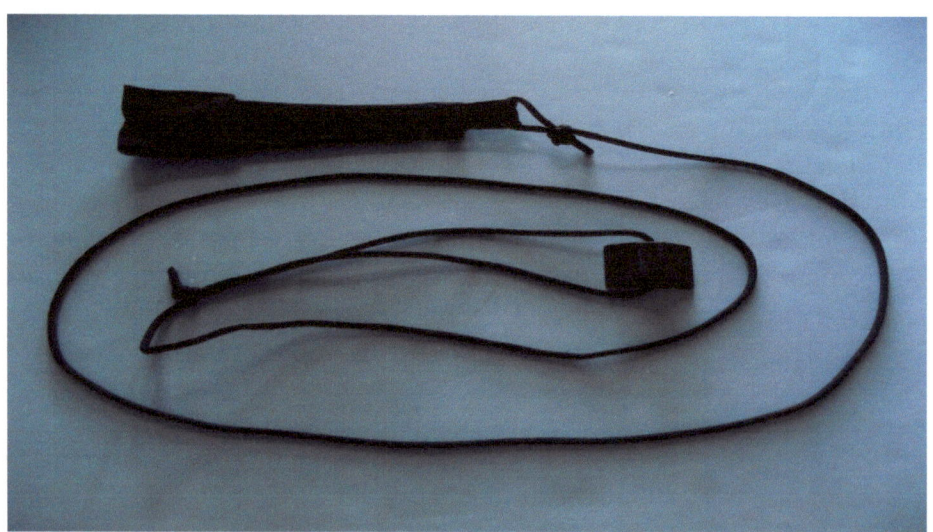

Selway Archery, Inc. Limb-Saver Recurve Bow Stringer

In the following chapter, we'll take a close look at two quality Muzzy bowfishing reels designed for the Muzzy Addict takedown recurve bow.

CHAPTER IX

BOWFISHING REELS & OTHER ESSENTIALS

Let's closely examine a pair of Muzzy bowfishing reels specifically designed for the Muzzy Addict recurve 40-pound draw weight takedown bow. They are the type of reel of which I'm sure many folks are familiar; that is, a spin-cast style fishing reel as opposed to the bottle-type container retriever reels found on other bowfishing setups.

The Muzzy model #1077-XD [Extreme Duty] Bowfishing Reel is a thumb-button operated spin-cast style that requires a Muzzy Anchor Bow Reel Seat Mount. The Muzzy model #1063 is simply a *combination* #1077-XD [Extreme Duty] Bowfishing Reel that comes packaged with a Muzzy Anchor Bow Reel Seat Mount. So don't be befuddled by thinking that the #1063 is a different model than the #1077-XD; it is not. The second reel we'll be examining closely is the Muzzy model #1069 XD Pro.

The Muzzy model #1069 XD Pro features an exclusive stainless steel mounting bracket affixed to the reel that screws into a bow's standard stabilizer insert and eliminates employing an anchor bow reel-seat mount. The #1069-XD Pro comes with mounting hardware for bracket-to-bow assembly, which is packaged up and underneath the easy-to-miss small cutout located at the bottom of the protective Styrofoam block: 5/16 x 25 machine screw, star-toothed lock washer, and common washer—all stainless steel, too. In lieu of the rear *button* on the #1077-XD, the #1069 XD Pro has a *lever* at the rear of the reel. This modification prevents the angler from inadvertently bumping the button and activating the free-spool or reel-in mode. Also, the integrated model #1069-XD Pro model reduces the overall weight of the reel when compared to the #1077-XD. Additionally, the new Muzzy #1069-XD Pro has been modified to form a more streamlined reel hood for smoother line flow. The reels come pre-spooled with 150 feet of 150-pound test Muzzy Braided Spectra Tournament Bowfishing Line, or in some cases, Muzzy Brownell Load Fast Flight Line. Braided Spectra fiber line is advertised as being seven feet per second faster than the Muzzy Brownell Load Fast Flight Line. The company strongly advises never to use braided Dacron line.

From left to right: Muzzy #1077-XD button-style type model; Muzzy #1069-XD Pro bracketed lever-style model. Center: hardware for the Muzzy #1069-XD Pro bracketed lever-style model

Shop around for these reels as some retailers charge considerably more for the same item(s). As with most spinning reels, the Muzzy XD spinning-style bowfishing reels come with right-hand retrieve. Converting over to left-hand retrieve is standard procedure. Instructions covering conversion, drag settings, tips for bow shooting, and operation come with each reel.

Both reels provide quality and value, incorporating an automotive-style disc drag system, stainless steel and brass drive system, and a stainless steel roller pick-up pin. Importantly, the two reels are saltwater rated. I suggest going with the Muzzy #1069-XD Pro for the advantages it has over the Muzzy #1077-XD. Of course, you could take either Muzzy XD reel and mount it to one of your vintage bows as discussed earlier. If and when upgrading, I suggest purchasing a recurve bow specifically designed for bowfishing. I highly recommend the Muzzy Addict recurve bow coupled to the Muzzy #1069-XD Pro reel.

Muzzy Addict recurve bow coupled to Muzzy model #1069-XD Pro bracketed bowfishing reel ~ Muzzy finger guards ~ Muzzy Mantis arrow rest

You can either snap shoot the Muzzy Addict recurve bow or come to a full draw controlled release. Keep in mind, though, that unlike most modern compound bows boasting 80–85 percent let-off, a traditional recurve bow has zero per cent let-off. But with only a 40-pound draw weight, this poses little problem. Agility is the name of the game. The Muzzy Addict recurve is a light bow, weighing in at approximately 3½ pounds *with* the Muzzy #1069-XD Pro bracketed reel attached! You can shoot this bow for hours on end without concern of fatigue. The bow features a magnesium riser and a non-slip soft-grip handle. You can shoot an arrow off the bow's shelf, utilize a Fish-Hook style rest, or select a Muzzy Mantis bowfishing shooting rest. I opted for the latter.

Muzzy Addict Bowfishing Bow ~ $169.99; Muzzy XD Pro Spin Style Reel (lever style model 1069) ~ $89.99; Bowfishing rest ~ $39.99. A Muzzy Bowfishing Kit is available for $199.99. Shop around.

Muzzy Mantis Bowfishing Rest

Also, you would absolutely want to utilize a pair of Muzzy's rubber glove-free finger guards, which is a string-release aid for those messy, slippery, wet conditions. As mentioned earlier, bowfishing can get quite messy. Staying with Muzzy components from the onset will ensure that all accouterments will fit properly from the get-go and save you frustration in the long run. A hairpin-style tool is included in the packaging to assist in sliding the pair of rubber guards (shorter and longer) onto the bowstring.

Muzzy Finger Guards and hairpin-style string tool

    Admittedly, this can be a bit of a chore because the instructions are not thorough. What you need to do first is wax the bowstring, particularly its lower end. Next, insert the hairpin-type tool onto the lower loop of the bowstring, right up the head of the pin. Why the lower loop? The answer is because the lower loop of the bowstring is a bit shorter than the upper loop and will, therefore, pass through the rubber finger guards easier when sliding and pulling the open end of the hairpin through the pair with pliers; first the shorter of the two finger-saver guards (top) then the longer one (bottom), working them up the bowstring and onto the server (middle green 7½-inch mid-section of the bowstring). You will have to pull strenuously with the pliers and push with your fingers to work the finger guards past the loop. You'll thank me later in that I saved you half the struggle by having you start on the shorter, smaller loop. After that point, it's pretty much a walk in the park.

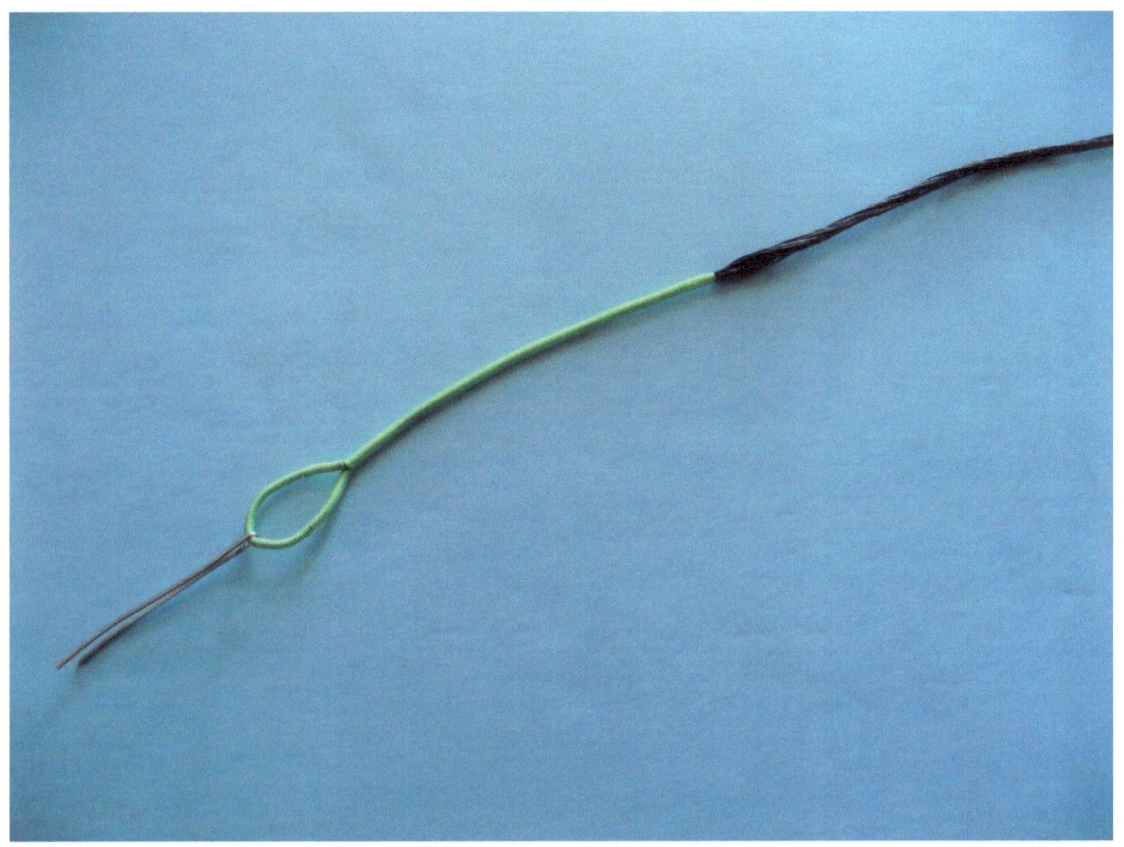

Shorter looped end of the Muzzy bowstring with tool for threading Muzzy Finger Guards

Do not concern yourself with adjusting the finger guards just yet. Simply get them onto the server somewhere around mid-point.

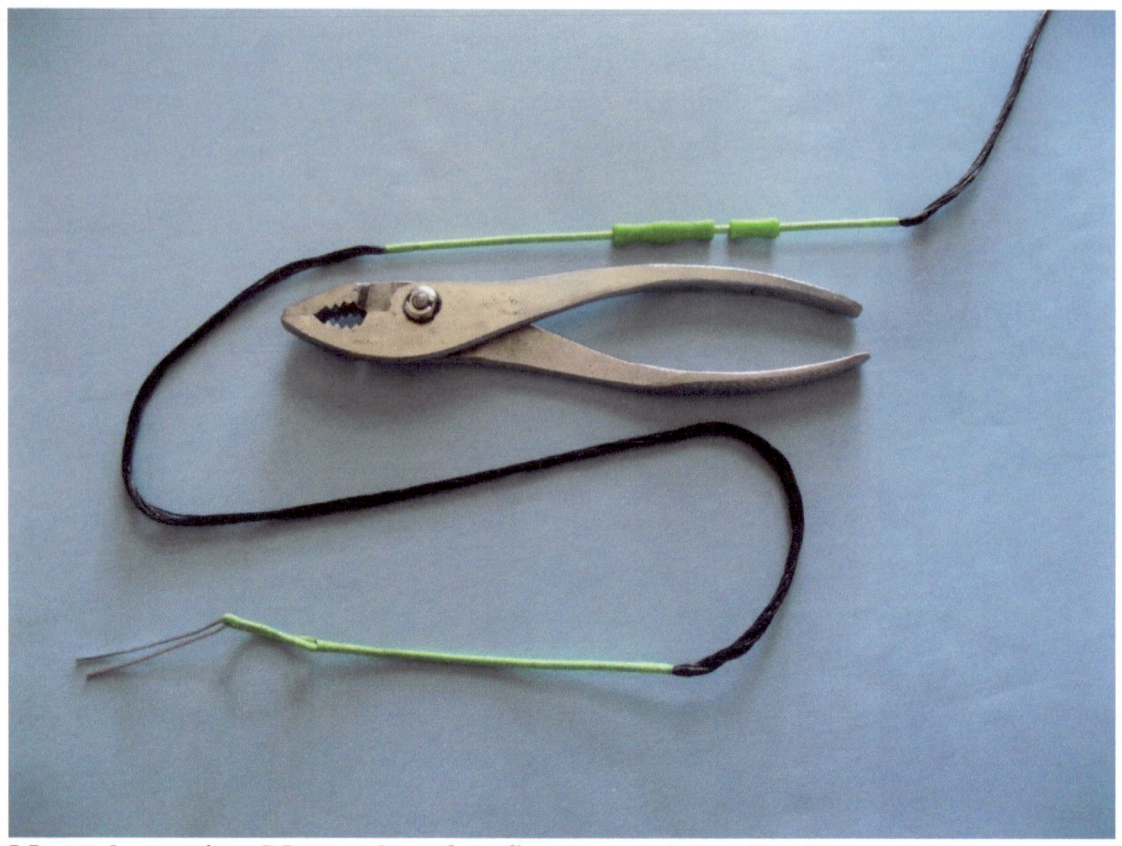

Muzzy bowstring, Muzzy glove-free finger guards, and tools

CHAPTER X

RIGGING AN ARROW FOR BOWFISHING ~ 'SWITCH-OUT' EXTENSION-CONNECTIONS

Let's move ahead to the Muzzy Classic 1020-CSS "Impale A Scale" Bowfish Arrow (overall length 34 inches inclusive of nock and 2½-inch Carp Point with Trocar Tip), which is a basic white 5/16-inch diameter shaft that boasts a reversible quick-release stainless steel Cam-Lock barb and an AMS safety slide. The arrow is designed to penetrate through tough-skinned fish. The barb reverses with two quick turns of the tip for easy fish removal. Shown below is the arrow shaft with green fly line attached [for illustration purposes only] so as to clearly depict the configuration of the laced loop wrapped around the top of the AMS Safety Slide, as well as the loop to connect line from arrow to reel.

Muzzy arrow shaft with line wrapped atop of AMS Safety Slide ~ $13.95

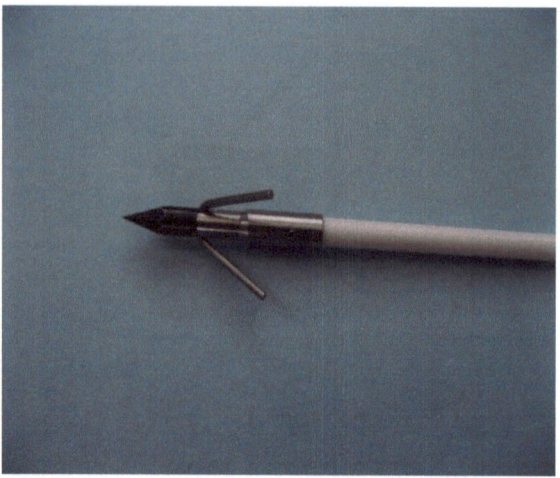

Muzzy arrowhead: Trocar tip & barb

There are several ways to tie line to the AMS safety slide. One is to first pull several feet of line from the reel with which to work. Form a 6-inch loop and tie a double overhand knot (surgeon's loop). From the top of the slide (side marked AMS), insert the loop down through either of the holes then up into the opposite hole. You'll note how neatly the double-laced line lies within the groove. Now comes the ostensibly tricky part; perhaps a bit difficult to follow here upon the printed page; easier to view on video. But not to worry, for the YouTube web page link with Mathew Shilling of AMS will help guide you through it: **www.youtube.com/watch?v=lM4lRnptNTk**

Mathew will demonstrate two ways to tie the line to the safety slide. I prefer his second method; however, you'll still insert the loop down through either of the holes from the *top* of the slide (side marked AMS ~ not the bottom of the slide as Mathew does) then up into the other hole as before. This way, the line still lays neatly in the groove.

After you've run the loop through the safety slide, pass the loop over the nock (rear) of the arrow, then run the slide all the way forward and over the head of the arrow (point and barb). Run the slide back up to the shock pad, pull tight, and you should have a perfect double-laced line secured within the groove of the safety slide. To remove the line, grab the loop's forward strand (facing the arrowhead) then run it down and over the head (point and barb), back up to shock pad then back over the nock. Pull, and the line will come free from the arrow.

My own design for quickly switching out arrows are two 5-inch loop-to-loop connections of 150-lb. test Spectra Line, joined together to form a handshake knot, no different than joining the loop at the end of a fly line to the loop of a leader. I then loop on a barrel swivel attached to a Tactical Angler (quick release) Power Clip, which comes in four sizes. The other end of the clip gets tied to the line from the reel by employing a clinch knot. Good to go.

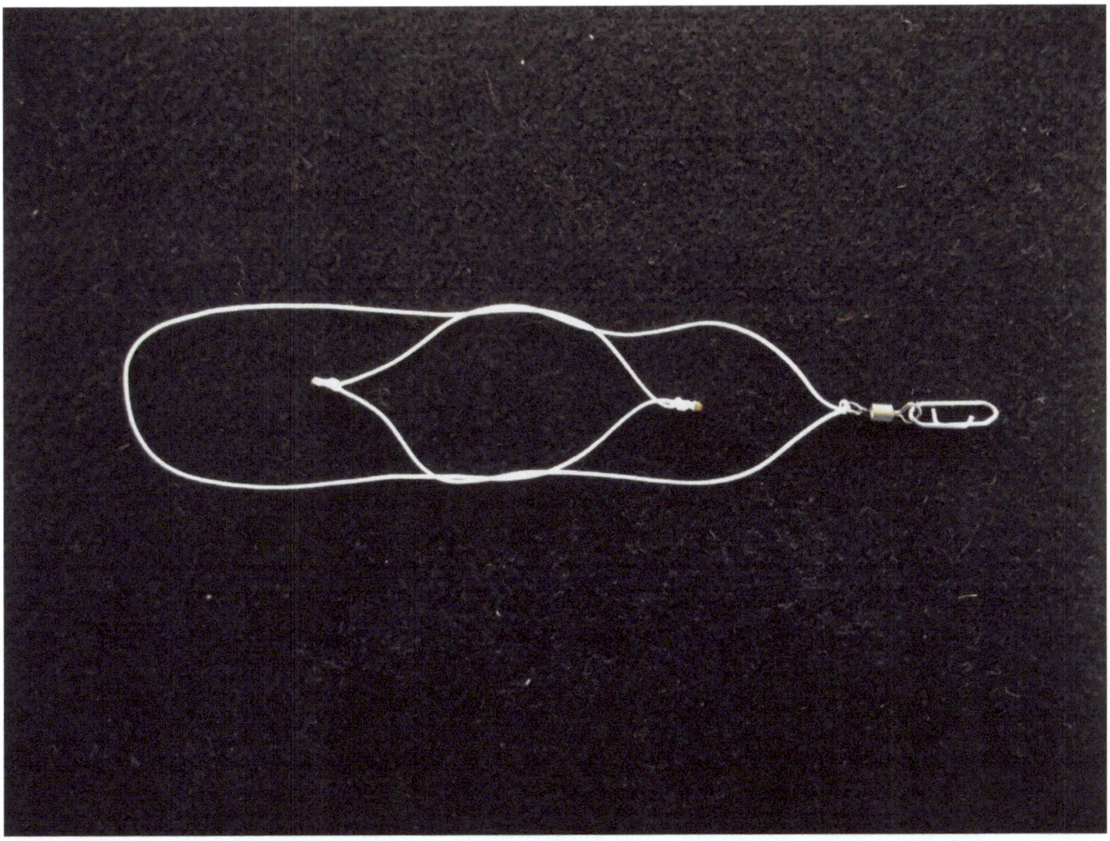

Loop-to-loop handshake knot ~ barrel swivel ~ Tactical Angler (quick release) Power Clip

Tactical Angler Power Clips are made from thick stainless steel wire, beefier than the standard round-ended clips with which you may be familiar. Also, these Power Clips are designed to be relatively pointed at both ends rather than rounded, and for two good reasons. They keep knots properly seated and barrel swivels better positioned.

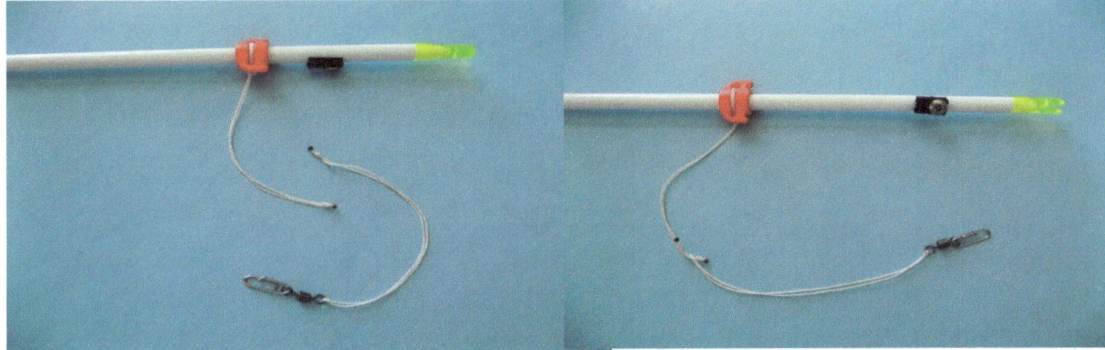

Left: Muzzy arrow shaft ~ AMS safety slide ~ shock pad ~ 'switch-out' connection extensions. Right: Arrow 'switch-out' extension-connection joined with loop-to-loop handshake knot

When tied properly, you'll note how neatly the double-laced line lies and will stay within the groove of the safety slide. To untie, push the knotted (burnt and sealed) ends of the handshake loop together, up and over the barrel swivel and clip. This is a quick way to switch out arrows.

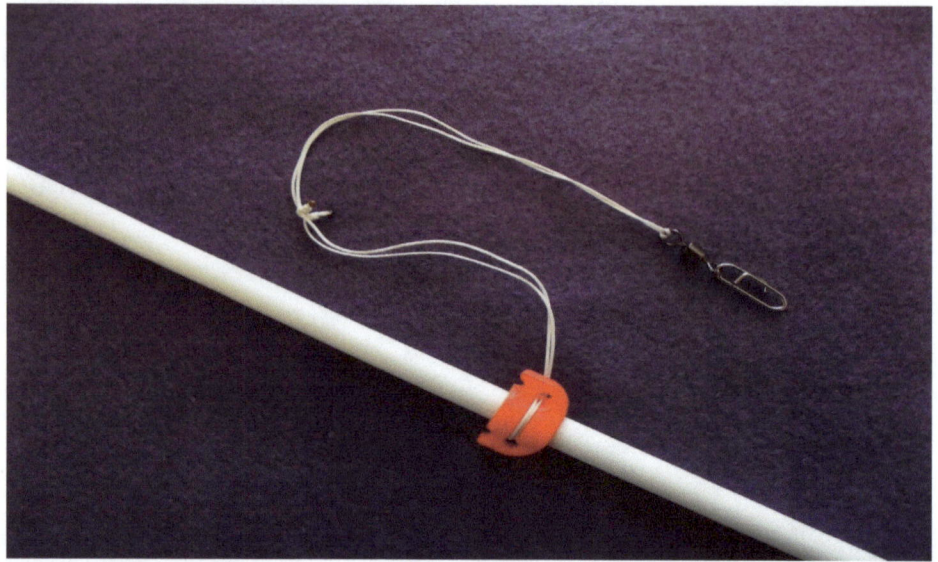

Bottom of AMS double-laced safety slide ~ loop-to-loop arrow extension connection ~ barrel swivel ~ Tactical Angler (quick release) Power Clip

Arrow 'Switch-Out' extension-connection loops ~ barrel swivel ~ Tactical Angler (quick release) Power Clip—all wrapped and secured to AMS safety slide via a small plastic cable tie for easy transportation

Complete bowfishing setup: Muzzy Addict recurve bow ~ bracketed Muzzy model #1069 XD Pro bowfishing spin-cast style reel ~ Muzzy Mantis arrow rest ~ Muzzy finger guards ~ Muzzy Classic "Impale A Scale" fiberglass arrow with safety slide ~ bow stringer—all good to go

For a bow <u>un</u>equipped with a quiver, a few 6-inch strips of ¾-inch wide Velcro brand self-grip strapping is perfect for securing arrows to bow while transporting. I also attach Selway's Limbsaver Recurve Bowstringer to the bow, inserting the bottom limb tip into the stringer's pocket (cup), bringing line, loop, and rubber block up toward the top limb before wrapping excess line around the upper limb as shown. Next, I insert a narrow quick-release cable tie through the hole in the rubber block and secure it to the limb. Everything is intact and ready to go: bow, arrows, 'switch-out' extension connections, and bow stringer. Note, too, that the Limbsaver is in its proper position and ready for easily stringing the bow—a nice advantage when setting up in predawn hours.

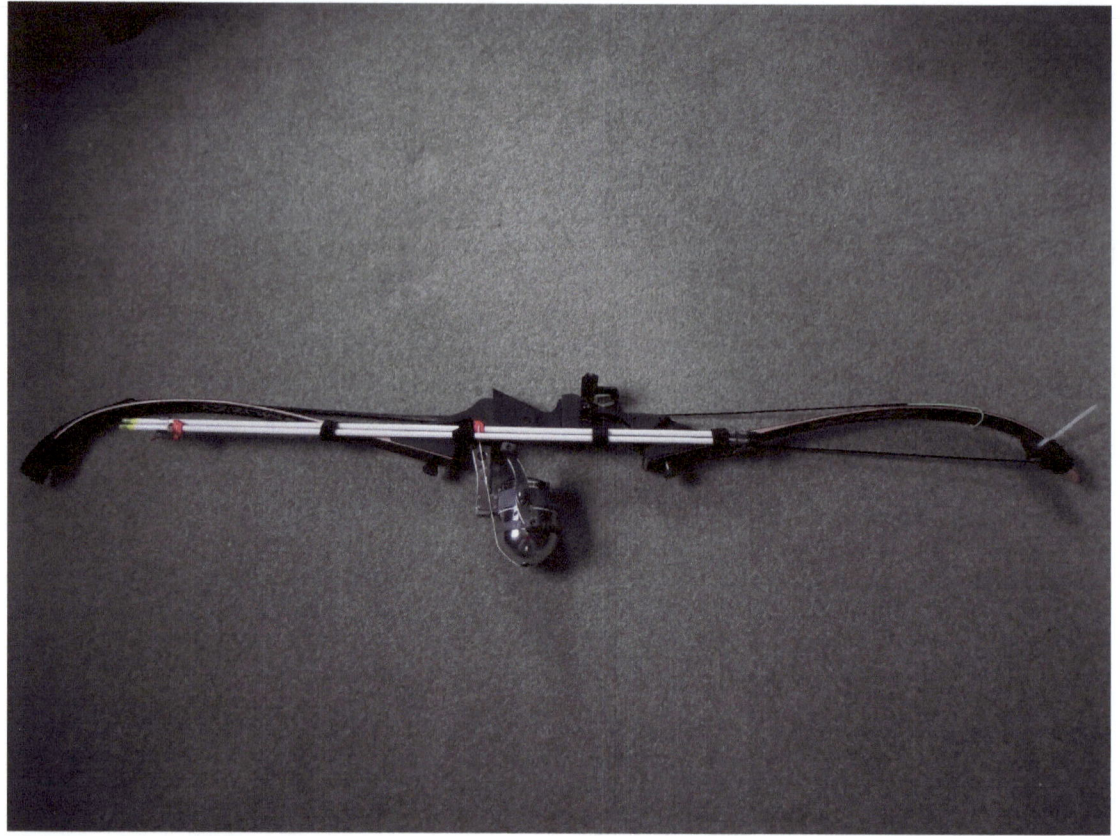

Velcro strips, cable tie to secure arrows and bow stringer while transporting

Bowfishing is a blast. It can either be done by walking the shoreline or slowly meandering along a body of water in a boat. In the following chapter, we'll take a close look at a couple of small boats that lend themselves well not only to bowfishing, but to crabbing, clamming, and light-duty inshore fishing. Additionally, we'll move along a lazy river in search of carp before concluding this chapter.

Mosquito Repellent Products

I don't want to be *bugged* when I'm fishing or hunting. Therefore, the Thermacell MR450 Mosquito Repellent product is a piece of equipment worth considering. A question of concern is the unit's effectiveness. A candid response is that it depends on whether or not there is a significant breeze to negate or limit its efficiency. In a calm setting, the unit works remarkably well, covering a 15 x 15 foot radius. To counter its limited effectiveness in a moderate wind, I spray my hat (not my skin) with OFF! Deep Woods insect repellent, which contains 25% Deet, or Repel Lemon Eucalyptus (Deet-free) repellent. Among these mosquito controls, I'm good to go. To keep my hands from being bitten up on extremely buggy days when angling, I also don a light pair of Dr. Shade 100% nylon fishing gloves (fingerless); they offer UV protection as well. Also, I lightly spray the backs of the gloves with repellent.

Thermacell MR450 Mosquito Repellent Product: unit, case, butane cartridge, mosquito repellent mat

When hunting from a treestand, I'm usually covered from head to foot with suitable clothing; however, if it's warm and buggy, I hang the Thermacell unit in its forest green case from a distant branch or hook behind me. The heat-activated mats are both Deet free and virtually scent free. I've never had an issue with odor as the treated mats [active ingredient: allethrum] mimic the smell of chrysanthemums. It *may* even help mask human odor, the bane of the deer hunter.

Although the unit has belt clips for convenient carry as illustrated, I do not wear the item as shown when angling, hunting, bowfishing, or lounging around a deck or patio. As a precautionary measure, I remove the unit and position it horizontally (for best results) upon a convenient surface a couple feet away, especially away from food and beverage. I have field-tested the item for well over a year. While relaxing on our back deck or neighbor's patio on a calm evening, this single unit has taken the place of a circular parade of citronella bucket candles. The unit provides 4 hours of protection before having to change the blue mat shown behind the protective screen. This is done in a matter of seconds. Simply slide in a new mat while pushing out the old. The butane cartridge is good for activating three mats; hence, you have 12 hours of protection before having to insert a new cartridge.

CHAPTER XI

BOATS & BEAUTY SURROUNDING BOWFISHING

Without breaking the bank, let's take a quick peek at a fine aluminum Tracker Topper 10-foot jon boat ($499) from which you can enjoy the sport of bowfishing. Keeping it simple is the key: KISS—Keep It Simple System—a mantra by which I live.

10 ft. aluminum Tracker jon boat ~ Muzzy Addict Recurve bowfishing setup

Early a.m. on the Peconic River, Riverhead, Long Island, New York

Most importantly, your first order of business before drawing back the bow is to make sure that the arrow's shock pad (bumper) is in the upright position, safety slide forward along the arrow shaft, and that the reel is in free-spool mode. You don't want the arrow flying off erratically. Going bowfishing your first time out with someone who is experienced is certainly sage advice.

Author aiming to take a carp

Dave Fulton on to a BIG carp

A common carp (Cyprinus carpio)

Left to Right: Author with friend and mentor, David Lee Fulton. Both men flaunt the same Muzzy setups: bows, reels, arrows, et cetera

Dave Fulton broke me into bowhunting for deer twenty-six years ago and more recently drew me into bowfishing. He is a consummate archer/hunter, having harvested deer out to 60 yards with a compound bow. Dave practices archery several times a week, point being that practice does, indeed, make perfect—or darn near it. Dave guided me (quite literally) along the shallow waters for bowfishing in the lower and upper reaches of the Peconic River in Riverhead, Long Island, New York. With either a compound bow for deer hunting, or a bowfishing outfit for carp, David is at home. He has taken sizable carp from the river, which the man knows like the back of his hand.

Referencing bowfishing, he modestly relates his successes and failures as bowfishing presents many challenges. Refraction (the bending of light as it passes from one medium into another) is but one of those challenges.

"Shoot four inches low for every foot of water," was David's mantra as I missed with my first, second, and third shot at some 5 and 6 pounders.

"It's not uncommon to see ten pounders around here, Bob," Dave said encouragingly. "Right around the bend by that dock over there, I think you'll see a couple of big guys; maybe 12 pounders. Remember, shoot four inches low for every foot of water. We'll be in about a foot or so. If you can't hit one of those big boys, there's that side of a barn over there by the horse. Maybe you can practice hitting the barn wall," he bantered.

I reminded David that he was my gillie for the day and to just keep rowing. He asked me if I had my sea legs, meaning that a sudden clumsy stroke from either oar could easily propel me from a standing position into a warm bath of water and vegetation. If not for bow and arrow in hand and at the ready, I might have welcomed David's not-so-subtle warning, for it was already a hot early July morning, and the sun was only beginning its ascent.

One of several impressive properties along a stretch (between lower and upper region) of the scenic Peconic River

On those long hot summer days while working a body of water, an electric motor is a blessing, offering a greater degree of stealth in lieu of clattery oars upon the surface and, consequently, spooking fish.

Minn Kota electric trolling motor

Let's take a quick peek at another boat that you can enjoy the sport of bowfishing. Again, keeping it simple is the key. If you are in the market for a truly portable, foldable, affordable boat for many on-the-water activities (angling, bowfishing, clamming, crabbing, et cetera), visit Porta-Bote at www.porta-bote.com. The 10'8" Porta-Bote sells for $2,699.

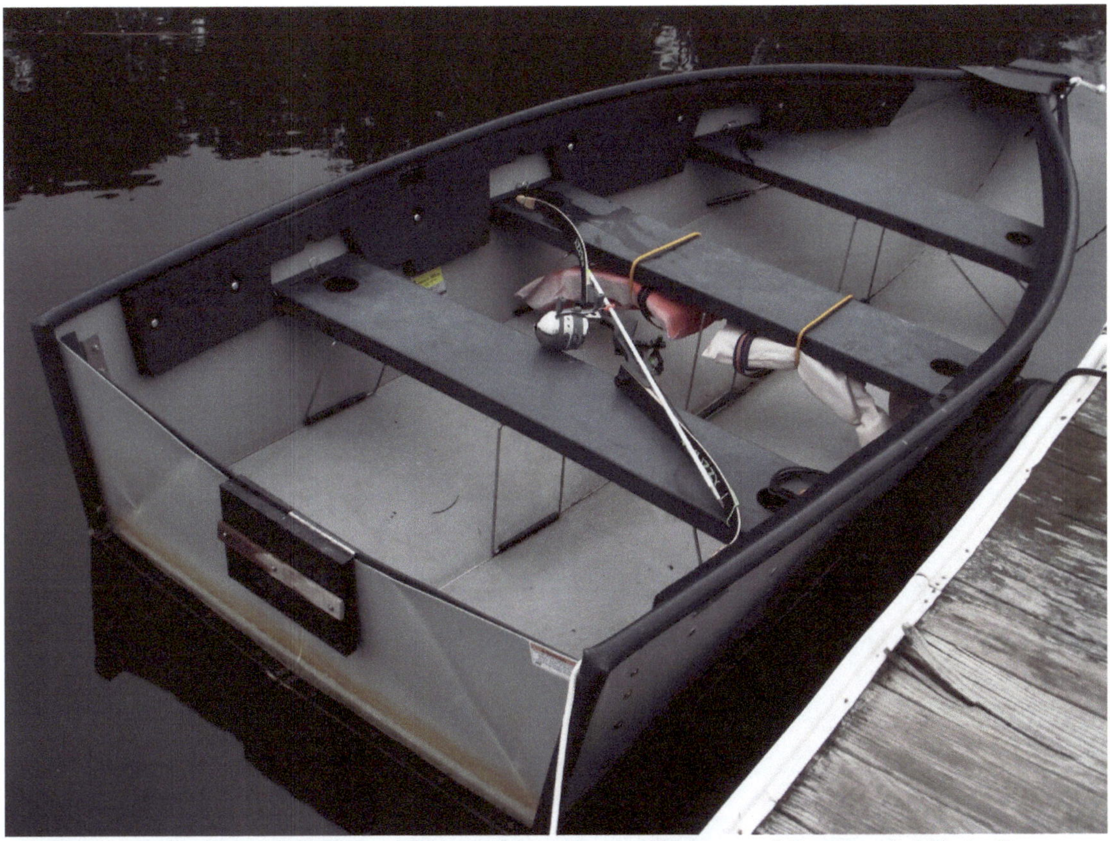

Author's 10 ft. foldable, affordable Porta-Bote ~ Muzzy Addict Recurve bowfishing setup

Foreground: Typical summer vegetation encountered bowfishing along the banks of the Peconic River

Lower stretch along the beautiful Peconic River

Ample Parking off of West Main Street in Riverhead ~ dirt road opposite Snowflake (ice cream shop)

I hope to see you on this gem of a river someday, bowfishing for BIG carp.

Acknowledgments

As a teenager in New Jersey, I hunted with a slug gun and continued my pursuit of deer with a gun through adulthood. When we moved to Riverhead, N.Y. in the early nineties, I met David Lee Fulton who introduced me to bowhunting. David is a consummate bowhunter who has traveled the country for big game. My sincere thanks go out to David for his tutelage and the many hours of fun we shared hunting deer with a bow and arrow. Years later, David initiated me into the challenging sport of bowfishing.

My gratitude also goes out to Christopher Paparo with whom I have also hunted. Chris, whose website is www.fishguyphotos.com, is an angler, hunter, falconer, photographer, and marine biologist. We shared good times together, and I learned much from the man.

Additionally, I want to thank all of the folks who worked with me regarding product and information support.

I am very fortunate to have a soulmate who loves the outdoors as much as I do. Although Donna does not hunt, she will, with camera in hand, assist me in the field. She supports all of my endeavors and makes our outdoor adventures a lot of fun. My love and gratitude always.

www.ingramcontent.com/pod-product-compliance
Lightning Source LLC
Chambersburg PA
CBHW041959150426
43194CB00002B/58